BrightRED Revision

Higher
PHYSICAL EDUCATION

Malcolm Thorburn

First published in 2008 by:
Bright Red Publishing Ltd
6 Stafford Street
Edinburgh
EH3 7AU

A CIP record for this book is available from the British Library

ISBN 978-1-906736-00-2

With thanks to:
The Partnership Publishing Solutions (layout) and Elaine Rowan (copy-edit)

Cover design by Caleb Rutherford – e i d e t i c

Illustrations by Armadillo Jam

Every effort has been made to seek all copyright holders. If any have been overlooked then Bright Red Publishing will be delighted to make the necessary arrangements.

The publishers would like to thank the following for permission to reproduce the following photographs: © Hulton Archive/Getty Images (p 20); © Hamish Blair/Getty Images Sport (p 21)

We would also like to thank the following for permission to reproduce material in this book: Telegraph Media Group Ltd for the extract 'Little fat chap a football giant' by David Miller in the *Daily Telegraph* of 19 November 2006; NI Syndication for the extract 'He came, he bowled, he conquered – Shane Warne' by Simon Barnes in *The Times* of 21 December 2006

Printed and bound in Scotland by Scotprint

CONTENTS

1 INTRODUCTION

SYLLABUS AND ASSESSMENT

BRIGHT RED REVISION!

This Bright Red Revision text is intended to help you review the design model for the Higher Physical Education course in a concise and digestible format. The text covers the important skills and concepts you will experience as you progress through your Higher course. If you can understand the information and approaches outlined in this book, then you will be well placed to tackle your Higher PE exam.

The text is organised to help support your learning as much as possible as you revisit your course experiences. From collecting information through to preparing for the end of course examination, this revision text will provide you with an accessible reference source.

Mind maps

To help you further understand how the course is arranged there are full revision mind maps at the back of this text (see Chapter 9). These mind maps provide you with an overview of the different key concepts included in the four areas of the Analysis and Development of Performance unit. The mind maps can also be found online at the Bright Red website (www.brightredpublishing.co.uk). These PDF files can be printed for you to use as you wish.

Other features of this book

- Don't forget
- Internet links
- Let's think about this...
- Key words
- Task

 One recommended website is www.bbc.co.uk/sport. Here, particularly in the Sport Academy section, you will find many different features on improving skills and techniques and on fitness and training, which might be useful for you to consider.

LET'S THINK ABOUT THIS

Keep in mind the following process as you progress through the text:

Learn by doing...   *...by reviewing...*   *...by thinking.*

SYLLABUS

A Higher course award consists of a Performance unit and an Analysis and Development of Performance unit.

> **To clarify the demands of the Higher course, visit this link at the Scottish Qualification Authority's website: http://www.sqa.org.uk/files_ccc/NQ_PE_Higher_Arrangements_Ed03_April05.pdf**
> **This Arrangements document for the Higher course contains useful information about the aims, objectives and methods of assessment. You will also find the grade descriptors, which are useful for describing the abilities you need to demonstrate to get the grade you want!**

Below is a more concise outline of the two Higher PE units.

Performance unit

In the **Performance unit** your highest performance marks in two activities count towards achieving a unit pass in Performance and to your overall course award. You are assessed by your teacher in the different activities in your course.

Analysis and Development of Performance unit

In the **Analysis and Development of Performance unit** you are required to progressively investigate performance, analyse performance, develop performance and evaluate performance. Chapters 2–8 explain, in detail, how this occurs and how you can make improvements.

DON'T FORGET

Analysis in Higher Level Physical Education is based on **your** own performance.

ASSESSMENT

At Higher level, Performance makes up 40% of your final mark and Analysis and Development of Performance 60% of your final mark. You can achieve a Course award with an 'A', 'B' or 'C' pass depending on your final mark. The Course assessment for Analysis and Development of Performance is by a written examination over two and a half hours. In this examination, you complete three answers from different areas of Analysis and Development of Performance.

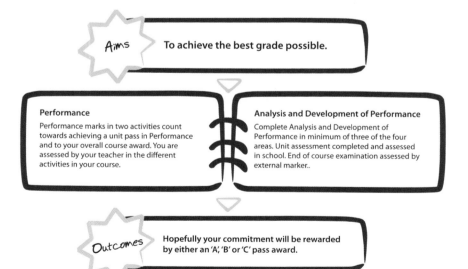

Aims — To achieve the best grade possible.

Performance

Performance marks in two activities count towards achieving a unit pass in Performance and to your overall course award. You are assessed by your teacher in the different activities in your course.

Analysis and Development of Performance

Complete Analysis and Development of Performance in minimum of three of the four areas. Unit assessment completed and assessed in school. End of course examination assessed by external marker..

Outcomes — Hopefully your commitment will be rewarded by either an 'A', 'B' or 'C' pass award.

LET'S THINK ABOUT THIS

There are four key stages involved in the Analysis and Development of Performance. You investigate performance, analyse performance, develop performance and evaluate performance.

HOW THIS TEXT WORKS

AN INTEGRATED APPROACH : BASKETBALL AND STRUCTURES, STRATEGIES AND COMPOSITION EXAMPLE

The example below shows the connections between your performance in basketball and your analytical understanding in Structures, Strategies and Composition. The example also highlights how being aware of this integrated learning connection can help you define your aims and meet your outcomes.

Aims
To improve my basketball performance and my understanding of Structures, Strategies and Composition.

Performance

Participate in small and full games to enable information about performance to be gathered.

Participating in various types of practices and small and full games in order to experience and understand more about Structures, Strategies and Composition.

Completing a specific Structures, Strategies and Composition based training programme in order to improve my overall basketball performance.

Participate in small and full games to enable evaluations of performance improvement to take place.

Analysis and Development of Performance

Investigate performance

Learning about how to gather information about performance.

Analyse performance

Learning through practical lessons about the three key concepts in Structures, Strategies and Composition

The structures, strategies and/or compositional elements that are fundamental to activities

Identification of strengths and weaknesses in performance in terms of: roles and relationships; formations; tactical and design elements; choreography and composition

Information processing, problem-solving and decision making when working to develop and improve performance.

Develop performance

Learning about how to monitor and review my performance and make any necessary adaptations to performance goals.

Evaluate performance

Learning how to compare and evaluate my performance improvement.

Outcomes
Improved basketball performance and increased understanding of Structures, Strategies and Composition.

UNDERSTANDING MORE ABOUT THE CYCLE OF ANALYSIS

The Cycle of Analysis is a widely-used approach for integrating performance with the analysis and development of your performance. As such, understanding more about the cycle of analysis should help you to review and evaluate your performance in greater detail.

The four stages of the Cycle of Analysis are:

1. investigate

2. analyse

3. develop

4. evaluate.

Note that the four stages link directly to the four learning outcomes involved in the Analysis and Development of Performance unit, namely: investigate performance, analyse performance, develop performance and evaluate performance.

Cycle of Analysis

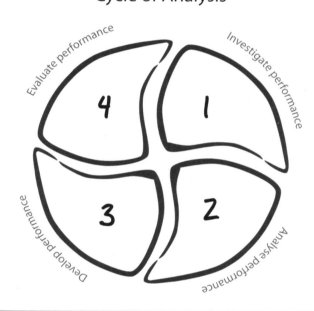

DON'T FORGET

It can be disheartening if you cannot see any apparent improvement in your performance (often referred to as reaching a learning plateau). Applying the Cycle of Analysis correctly can help you avoid this occurring.

LET'S THINK ABOUT THIS

For the activities in your course, you should be able to outline how they are integrated with different areas of analysis and development of performance. Review your course plans for Investigating, Analysing, Developing and Evaluating performance. When will this occur for the different practical activities in your course?

REVIEWING METHODS OF COLLECTING INFORMATION

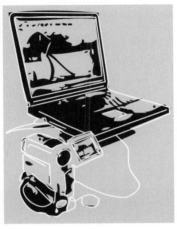

Recall

In order to carry out a thorough review of your performance, you must collect relevant and detailed information. This information must be specific to:

- the nature and demands of the activity
- your role and responsibilities within the activity
- your current level of performance
- the area of Analysis and Development of Performance being investigated.

Your aim is to analyse how you collected information (data) and why the methods used for collecting information were valid. This then makes it possible for you to investigate further your performance strengths and weaknesses and development needs. As such, the purpose of collected information is to provide you with a record of your performance to which you can make further, regular references.

Within your record of performance it is often important to have a balance between quantitative (objective, clearly measurable information) and qualitative (subjective, opinion-based information) as this helps you to develop depth in your answers. Consider the following example from basketball where information has been collected about passing effectiveness in a small-sided basketball game.

DON'T FORGET

Ensure your own performance is the focus of analysis review at Higher level.

DON'T FORGET

Analysis in Higher Level Physical Education is based on **your** own performance.

COLLECTING INFORMATION IN BASKETBALL

Basketball game	Objective	Subjective
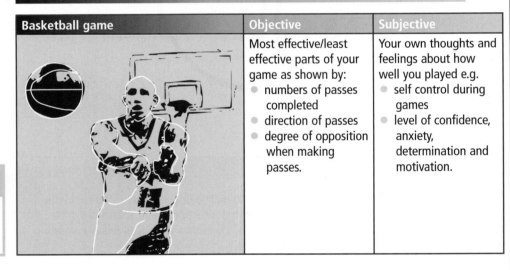	Most effective/least effective parts of your game as shown by: • numbers of passes completed • direction of passes • degree of opposition when making passes.	Your own thoughts and feelings about how well you played e.g. • self control during games • level of confidence, anxiety, determination and motivation.

In this example the combination of objective and subjective information adds depth to your explanation e.g. by explaining how making effective and ineffective passes affected your level of confidence throughout the game.

If your data is purely objective or subjective, e.g. concentrating on just the number and direction of the passes or by only considering your thoughts and feelings, less detail is available.

MATCHING PERFORMANCE QUALITIES WITH VALID METHODS OF COLLECTING INFORMATION

Described below are two feasible examples of valid methods for collecting information which link effectively to swimming at a Higher performance level. Your performance aim is to 'demonstrate effective performance in challenging contexts' by developing your repertoire (range) of skills and techniques, decision-making and control and fluency. When collecting information about your swimming performance, it is important that it relates to these types of performance qualities.

Swimming and preparation of the body

Performance demands:

● **Repertoire:** You should be competent in most of the key elements of front crawl. This should be shown in your body position, leg action, arm action, breathing and timing.

● **Decision-making:** The performance of front crawl should be in demanding contexts where the key elements of each stroke are sustained during the swim. This should be reflected in the interval times taken.

● **Control, fluency:** In front crawl, the body position should be streamlined with the leg action alternating and continuous, balancing the movements of the arms.

Central Academy: Higher Level Physical Education: Observation Schedule

Performance Context: Swimming 200 m (8 × 25 m lengths) in order to measure ability to sustain swimming performance in demanding contexts. Review observation schedule results as measured by classmate following swim and repeat assessment of performance at middle and end of training programme.

Table 2.1 is an example observation schedule for swimming.

Distance	Stroke quality	Pulse check*	Interval time	Cumulative time
1				
2 50 m	Legs ✓ Arms ✓	140	1.06	1.06
3				
4 100 m	Legs ✓ Arms?	150	1.12	2.18
5				
6 150 m	Legs ✓ Arms?	160	1.20	3.38
7				
8 200 m	Legs? Arms ✗	160	1.26	5.04

Table 2.1 Example observation schedule

The stroke quality responses can be interpreted as follows:

Checklist markings	
✓ = highly effective	**Leg action:** Extended leg kick which is effective in maintaining streamlining **Arm action:** High arm recovery and regular strong catch and pull
? = limited effectiveness	**Leg action:** Mostly extended leg kick with slight leg roll causing disturbance **Arm action:** Arm recovery usually gaining strong catch and pull
✗ = ineffective	**Leg action:** Uncomfortable leg roll with knee bend causing disturbance **Arm action:** Wide arm recovery with indistinct catch and pull
*Pulse check information: After swimming two lengths (50 m), pause, measure pulse quickly for 6 seconds (timed from pool clock or stopwatch) and multiply by 10 to calculate approximate pulse time per minute.	

contd

Swimming and skills and techniques

Performance demands:

- **Repertoire:** There should be little loss of momentum as the body completes turns.
- **Decision-making:** Key elements of each stroke are sustained during the swim.
- **Control, fluency:** The timing should be smooth, balanced and constant.

Central Academy: Higher Level Physical Education: Observation Schedule
Performance Context: Swimming widths in 8 m wide pool in order to increase frequency of turns. Complete five turns, rest and recover. Repeat on a further two occasions, then review observation schedule results as measured by classmate.

Skill: Turning   **Technique:** Tumble turn

Table 2.2 provides an example observation schedule for tumble turn technique development.

Essential features		Self check 1	Self check 2
Preparation • Swim towards wall at controlled speed • Adjust arm action cycle to begin turn at correct point and with preferred lead arm			
Action • Initiate turn as leading arm sweeps across body • Pull hips forward and forward somersault • Tuck head in tight • Place feet on the wall approximately half a metre below water surface • Push off the wall and twist onto your front (if swimming front crawl) • Extend arms forward to aid streamlining as you drive from wall	 		
Recovery • Keep arms forward to maintain streamline shape during recovery • Begin leg kick and arm action as you surface			

Table 2.2 Tumble turn

Checklist markings can be interpreted as follows.

Checklist markings	
✓ = highly effective	Retains momentum during turns, sustains overall swimming speed, timing is smooth, fluent and controlled
? = limited effectiveness	Some loss of momentum during turns, swimming speed slightly slows as a result, timing is mostly smooth, fluent and controlled
✗ = ineffective	Noticeable loss of momentum during turns, speed slows considerably during turns, timing is a little jerky as large body movements lack fluency and control

LET'S THINK ABOUT THIS

The two observation schedules above can be completed either by yourself as performer, by a classmate or by your teacher.

OBSERVATION SCHEDULES

Recall

Both swimming examples have used observation schedules to collect information. Observation schedules, in general, have the following advantages.

- They enable observation criteria to be established which can measure your performance qualities and identify your analysis needs.

- The evidence you gain from performance is **valid**, **reliable** and **straightforward to interpret**.

- They enable you to retain a record of your performance.

- They allow you to make later repeated observations of your performance for comparative purposes.

- Observations of performance can be used for either collecting information about a single technique, fitness over a period of time or effectiveness in a game.

  Key words: accuracy, validity, reliability, objectivity

OTHER METHODS OF COLLECTING INFORMATION

There are various other methods available for collecting information. These include: videos of performances; reflections on your performance; using a dictaphone; knowledge of results; error detection/correction; and game analysis.

DON'T FORGET

Your review should focus on **why** the methods of information you used on your course to collect information about your performance were effective.

VIDEO OF PERFORMANCES

Video recording of performances has the following advantages.

- It allows more **accurate** observation of the movements in the performance.

- When performances occur at speed, slow-motion replay is the best way to assess accurately what actually happened.

- Repeated observation and replays of key events become possible.

- **Detailed** analysis of technique becomes possible when fast, complicated movements are slowed down.

Remember that good camera position and angles are vital for obtaining detailed and useful video information.

DON'T FORGET

Making a video recording of your performance will enable you to complete the observation schedule yourself.

PERSONAL REFLECTIONS ABOUT YOUR PERFORMANCE

- Reflect on how you feel about your performance. In many settings, e.g. dance, your emotions affect your performance. Use this subjective evidence to reflect critically on your performance.

- Sometimes subjective evidence is as useful as objective results.

- Record your thoughts and emotions, e.g. in a performance diary. Which emotional mind-set helps generate your best performance?

- Replay and re-imagine your performance and consider how to enhance it.

- A well-designed questionnaire can also help record your thoughts and reflections on key performance issues.

Key words: critical reflection, subjectivity

USING A DICTAPHONE

Using a dictaphone has the following advantages.

- Using a dictaphone can help you collect your thoughts and impressions quickly and easily.

- You can use it before, during and after a game or activity.

- The tape can be replayed at will.

ERROR DETECTION/CORRECTION

A major goal of performance review is to discover if your performance is developing and if you are reaching new skill levels. Ask yourself,

- Are you using a broader range of techniques?

- Is your performance becoming more fluent and controlled?

- Is your decision-making improving?

Continuous review, alone or with teachers and coaches, will identify if your performance has specific errors. Once accurately identified, you can work towards eliminating them from your performance.

Ensuring that the performance criteria you select match the features of performance requiring review is crucial for accurate error detection and for identifying correction remedies.

DON'T FORGET

Error detection/correction is an important method of collecting information for high level performers as well as lesser able performers. This is because even high-level performers might have some skills and techniques weaknesses in their performance. For example, some very talented strikers in football might still be quite weak at skills which they use less often e.g. tackling.

LET'S THINK ABOUT THIS

Remember that the specific errors which you might have in your performance will often change. For example, in golf it may be that your short iron game contains some technical weaknesses. Once these have been addressed, other performance improvements are likely to be required e.g. putting.

KNOWLEDGE OF RESULTS

Knowledge of results is a valuable method of investigating performance. It can be used in all four areas of Analysis and Development of Performance.

Tennis example (serving)

Performance Appreciation: The service information could provide knowledge about some of the special challenges associated with serving. For example, how satisfied are you that 2 of 30 first serves were aces? How does this compare with previous performance results? Would you have expected more? To what extent did the performance abilities of your opponent influence results?

Preparation of the Body: Tennis serving can become physically tiring as the major muscle groups are repeatedly required to work together to produce a strong service action. In this match, 60 serves were made. Reviewing information about the depth of your serves might indicate whether fatigue adversely affected your serve as the game progressed. (The speed of your serves would be another form of knowledge of results which could be useful for investigating your performance.)

Skills and Techniques: The service information could be used to review the accuracy of your serves. For example, nearly half of first serves were 'out' and 46% (28 out of 60) serves were second serves. What do these results indicate about serving accurately during games? Is it necessary to compromise a little on the speed of serve in order to increase the number of first serves landing 'in'?

DON'T FORGET

Ensure your knowledge of results links feasibly to the area of analysis and development of performance being investigated.

Structures, Strategies and Composition: The service information could be used to review whether your serves matched the service strategies chosen for playing against your opponent. For example, 10 first serves on the forehand side were served out wide (right hand side of service reception box) while only 5 first serves on the forehand side were served nearer to the centre line of the court. However, 2 of these 5 serves were aces (point won outright). Would it have been better to have served to this part of the court more often, given that none of the 10 first serves to the right hand side of the service reception box were aces?

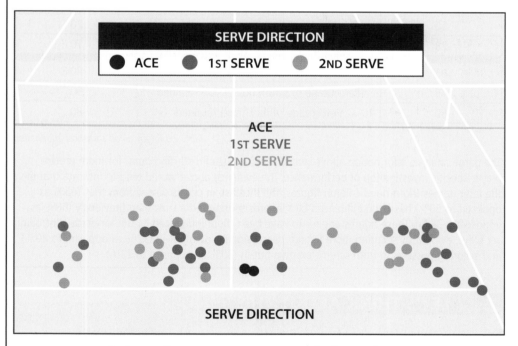

Service reception area
Backhand (right handed)

Service reception area
Forehand (right handed)]

GAME ANALYSIS

Statistical analysis of the actions in a game can be used to measure and analyse performance. In the rugby union example in Table 2.3 below, a range of game-related statistical information enables a comparison of the first 5 matches with the second set of 5 matches played.

1st XV: Information from first five matches		1st XV: Information from matches six to ten
50	Percentage of points from tries	65
25	Percentage of points from penalty goals	15
20	Percentage of points from conversions	15
5	Percentage of points from drop goals	5
4.0	Tries per game (average)	5.5
3.0	Penalty goals per game (average)	2.0
0.5	Drop goals (average)	0.5
35	Percentage of tries scored by forwards	50
65	Percentage of tries scored by backs	50
20	Percentage of tries from lineout possession	32
22	Percentage of tries from scrum possession	30
12	Percentage of tries from penalties/free kicks	8
18	Percentage of tries from turnover/errors	20
28	Percentage of tries from opponents' kicks	10
65	Percentage of lineout possession retained	80
75	Percentage of scrum possession retained	90
80	Percentage of ruck/maul retained	80

Table 2.3 Rugby union statistical information

The game analysis information above would provide a useful starting point for more precise player-specific investigation of performance. The evidence above would tend to indicate that in the later games (right-hand column figures) the increase in points scored from tries (65% as opposed to 50%) has been influenced by forwards scoring more tries than previously (50% as opposed to 35%). These figures appear to have been more influenced by the forwards controlling set plays, evident by securing more lineout possession on own put-in (32% as opposed to 20%) and securing possession from scrums on own put-in (30% as opposed to 22%).

LET'S THINK ABOUT THIS

Most of the methods described for collecting information can be used in any of the four areas of Analysis and Development of Performance provided they are linked to your precise practical performance needs. Choose investigative methods which allow you to describe accurately what you did when performing. You can then explain why your methods of collecting information were suitable.

3 REVIEWING HOW TO ANALYSE YOUR PERFORMANCE: PERFORMANCE APPRECIATION

THE FOUR AREAS OF ANALYSIS AND DEVELOPMENT OF PERFORMANCE

1. Performance Appreciation (this chapter)

2. Preparation of the Body (Chapter 4)

3. Skills and Techniques (Chapter 5)

4. Structures, Strategies and Composition (Chapter 6).

Recall

- Your Analysis and Development of Performance includes the study of at least three of these areas.

- Each of the areas of Analysis and Development of Performance is made up of a number of Key Concepts.

- Area 1 Performance Appreciation takes a broad perspective on performance. Areas 2, 3 and 4 look at specific aspects of performance. (See diagram below.)

DON'T FORGET

For many students this is the most challenging part of completing the cycle of analysis. Try to ensure your revision focuses on understanding as much as possible about the Key Concepts.

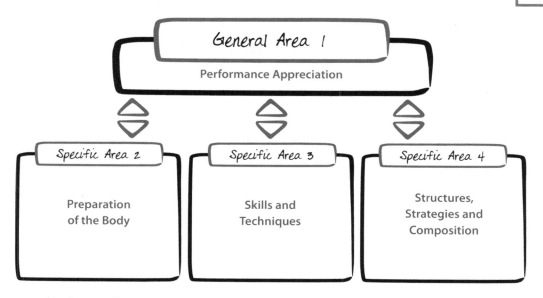

- This diagram illustrates the links between Performance Appreciation and Areas 2, 3 and 4.

- When analysing key concepts in Performance Appreciation, consider their relationship to key concepts in Areas 2, 3 and 4.

- When studying Areas 2, 3 or 4, links should be made with the key concepts in Performance Appreciation.

DON'T FORGET

You must keep in mind that often your Analysis and Development of Performance coursework will require you to connect your general understanding of the course to specific examples, and vice versa.

LET'S THINK ABOUT THIS

In your Analysis and Development of Performance work, it is important that you do not make links **across** the three specific areas. Links are made from Area 1 to Areas 2, 3 and 4 and vice versa. Try not to discuss key concepts from across the three specific areas together as this will lead to a lack of precision in your explanations about analysis and development of performance.

KEY CONCEPT 1: THE OVERALL NATURE AND DEMANDS OF QUALITY PERFORMANCE

THE NATURE OF PERFORMANCE

Some general factors influencing performance preferences are listed in Table 3.1.

DON'T FORGET

In this key concept you examine in detail the nature of quality performance and the different demands on performance.

Special nature: **competing in public**		I really like special occasions when we play competitive games in front of many spectators.
Special nature: **performing in public**		Performing in front of an audience adds to the magic of the occasion and makes for a special atmosphere.
Quality focus: **group control**		When synchronised swimming, I enjoy contributing to the different parts of our routine where the focus is on making controlled and precise movements.
Quality focus: **individual control**		In golf, I like being responsible for my own performance, selecting shots and trying different strategies.
Special challenges: **feeling of new adventure**		When kayaking in white water I enjoy the challenge of controlling the kayak in the fast-moving rapids.
Experiential nature: **trying something new**		I had never tried baseball before, but it was fun and something new to do.

Table 3.1 Performance preferences

 **LET'S THINK ABOUT THIS**

Review the table above with a classmate. Share your performance preferences and complete a similar table of your own.

THE DEMANDS OF PERFORMANCE

Factors influencing a preference for individual as opposed to group activities and for competitive rather than non-competitive activities are listed in Table 3.2.

Individual, team and group activities		Competitive and non-competitive activities	
I prefer doubles badminton games as I enjoy working as part of a team and sharing attacking and defending responsibilities.		I like non-competitive activities such as gym-based fitness sessions where you can meet other people socially and have an enjoyable time.	
I prefer singles badminton games as I like to be able to select attacking and defending strategies and change these during games as necessary.		I like individual competitive activities such as orienteering where you can test yourself against other competitors and enjoy the satisfaction of knowing you have tried your very best.	
I prefer activities such as dance where we discuss and suggest improvements as part of a group.		I like competitive team activities the most. At the start of a game of basketball we get in a circle and encourage each other to demand the best performance possible.	

Table 3.2 Individual/team/group and competitive/non-competitive preferences

LET'S THINK ABOUT THIS

Referring to the table above, review your own preferences for individual, team and group activities and competitive and non-competitive activities. Give your reasons why you prefer the nature and demands of the activities you have identified.

KEY CONCEPT 2: TECHNICAL, PHYSICAL, PERSONAL AND SPECIAL QUALITIES OF PERFORMANCE

DON'T FORGET

For this key concept, you need to focus on the special, personal, technical and physical qualities required to appraise the strengths and weaknesses of individual, team or group performance.

QUALITIES OF PERFORMANCE

Special qualities include inventiveness, expression, flair and creativity.

Personal qualities include competitiveness, determination, sense of fairness and courage.

Technical qualities include rhythm, fluency, consistency, timing, control, refinement and effectiveness.

Physical qualities include strength, power, dynamism, light and speed.

LET'S THINK ABOUT THIS

As your appreciation of performance develops, analyse the role of different qualities involved in your performance overall, whether in individual, team or group activities.

Individual activity: *Golf*

Special: The golfer shows creativity with different approach shots to the green. Changes in the shape of the swing can lead to different flight trajectories designed to achieve either backspin or for the ball to run along the ground towards the pin.

Personal: The golfer shows a sense of fairness when marking their ball and recording shots taken.

Technical: The golfer shows refinement and control in maintaining the fluency and consistency of their golf swing.

Physical: The golfer shows a lightness of touch when playing difficult shots, for example, shots in and around bunkers.

Team activity: *Volleyball*

Special: The volleyball player is able to express her ability by having the confidence to attempt an attacking spike shot.

Personal: All the volleyball players are competitive. All the players in blue are active in defence and the support players in white are watching to see whether they are required if the spike shot is blocked.

Technical: To play the spike shot the volleyball player requires rhythm, fluency, timing and control.

Physical: All the volleyball players jumping at the net require power and the other players require speed as they need to react quickly.

contd

QUALITIES OF PERFORMANCE contd

Group activity: *Modern dance*

Special: The dancers show imagination, flair and creativity through improvising (making up) a jump in their performance.

Personal: The dancers show an ability to work together by moving into position to complete the jump.

Technical: The dancers show movement control, poise and refinement when completing the jump.

Physical: The dancers possess strength in the leg muscles to initiate the jump.

LET'S THINK ABOUT THIS

Review and explain the technical, physical, personal and special qualities of performance you have encountered while undertaking the various activities in your course.

TASK

Read and review the two articles below to develop a more detailed appreciation of quality performance. The first example is an obituary of the famous footballer, Ferenc Puskas, and highlights how he possessed the type of technical, physical, personal and special qualities required of a top sportsperson. The second article is about cricketer Shane Warne.

'Little fat chap' a football giant
by David Miller,
Daily Telegraph, 19/11/2006

'Great footballers generate respect, admiration, occasionally astonishment. Ferenc Puskas, unsurpassed Hungarian of an arguably unsurpassed national team who died aged 79, above all inspired fear among opponents. He was, unquestionably, the most lethal marksman of all time, the instantaneous power and accuracy of his shooting as venomous as a serpent's tongue. For supremacy, within a team sport, no performer in his prime has matched Puskas in modern times except, perhaps, the cricketer Don Bradman.

Other great players such as Pele, Alfredo di Stefano, Diego Maradona and Johan Cruyff may have exerted more refined tactical influence upon their teams, but statistics show that Puskas was the executioner par excellence. In 84 matches for Hungary, he scored 83 times. He was also top scorer four times in the Hungarian League between 1947 and 1954, then four times in five Spanish League seasons he was the leading scorer having moved to Real Madrid after the Hungarian uprising of 1956.

With Real, he scored 156 goals in 180 games in La Liga – with another 35 goals in 39 European Cup appearances – before retiring in 1967, aged 40. With his squat figure, barely 5 ft 7 in and crucial low centre of gravity, and with powerful thighs like Maradona's, he needed little back-lift to produce power in his left foot. Having small feet and striking the ball dead centre, his shooting was devastating. He could, uniquely, generate Steven Gerrard-like power even when standing stationary.

contd

19

Before the famous England–Hungary game in 1953, England had been scornful of these Communist state-sponsored "amateurs", even though they had been Olympic champions the year before and were undefeated in three seasons. They had referred beforehand in the dressing-room to Puskas with his characteristically protruding tummy as "that little fat chap".

Later Puskas joined Real Madrid and Di Stefano, already three times champions of the new European Cup. Puskas, now 32, won his first and Real Madrid fourth European title, and then came that unforgettable match at Hampden Park in 1960. Eintracht Frankfurt were no simpletons, having torn Rangers apart in an earlier round, yet now Real, in the most glorious form with Puskas scoring four times and Di Stefano three, shredded the Germans in a 7-3 victory. Puskas belonged to that special class of striker, including Jimmy Greaves, Gerd Muller of West Germany, and Maradona who would have the ball in the net at close range before the goalkeeper could blink, such was their anticipation. It is often said wrongly of those who have been exceptional that their like will not be seen again, but in the case of Ferenc Puskas, it is true.'

Some examples of performance qualities are listed below. You may have identified others.

- An example of technical quality is 'Having small feet and striking the ball dead centre, his shooting was devastating'.
- An example of physical quality is 'With his squat figure, barely 5 ft 7 in and crucial low centre of gravity, and with powerful thighs like Maradona's, he needed little back-lift to produce power in his left foot'.
- An example of personal quality would be that Ferenc Puskas showed the dedication necessary to keep playing competitive football at the highest levels until 40 years old.
- An example of special quality is 'Puskas belonged to that special class of striker, including Jimmy Greaves, Gerd Muller of West Germany, and Maradona who would have the ball in the net at close range before the goalkeeper could blink, such was their anticipation'.

He came, he bowled, he conquered

by Simon Barnes,
The Times, 21/12/2006

'Michael Jordan was at his very best when I saw him and it has stayed with me across the years, especially when I turn to that absorbing and elusive subject of greatness. Jordan was playing for the Chicago Bulls against the Phoenix Suns in the NBA finals in Chicago in 1993. In the second game, Jordan scored 55 points in a virtuoso display of sporting greatness. And Paul Westphal, the Suns coach, was asked if he was surprised by what Jordan did. "No. I'm amazed, but I'm not surprised." He then added: "He inflicted his will on us". Now, as Shane Warne is to retire from Test-match cricket, these words come back to me. That is because they are peculiarly suitable for Warne.

Ever since he established himself as a match-winning bowler, Warne has constantly amazed me, never once surprised me. And in match after match he has inflicted his will on his opponents, the last of whom was England. They lost that traumatic second Test in Adelaide for one simple reason – the will of Shane Warne. Warne is the

contd

finest bowler of any kind ever to play cricket. He was the only bowler named by the great and the good of the sport when they listed their five cricketers of the 20th century, and there hasn't been another to emerge since.

Warne has done what Jordan has done. Both played a team game with outstanding individual brilliance, without once ceasing to be a team player through and through. Both loved the cosiness of the team but loved to be the stand-out man within it. Both thrived on responsibility. Both loved to be the man expected to make the crucial contribution to victory.

In times of trouble, in times of strength, these were the men who stepped forward. Each used his team as a kind of court, the better to set off his greatness, but did so without ever losing the corporate buzz of team sports, the rejoicing in a colleague's accomplishments, the relishing of achievement as a shared thing.

I loved that storming performance of Jordan's against the Suns – the way he demanded the ball, the way he forced those around him to play above their abilities, the way his opponents were forced to go along with Jordan's desire. I saw the same thing with Warne. You can isolate the individual tricks of brilliance: Jordan's no-look pass, that move when he fakes right and goes right, the way he still has half a dozen options after he has taken off. And you can pick out the various weapons in Warne's armoury: the flipper, the newly revived googly and the leg break that turns square on a sheet of glass.

But above all, with both of them, you remember the command. The command of space and time; each player's certainty that the moment belonged to him. I saw Jordan, motionless, ball in his enormous hands, waiting until the time was absolutely right – and then the plunge into the maelstrom of bodies, the pass or the fake, the run and drive, sometimes to defy three markers and score, sometimes to take them out of the game and open the way for a colleague to finish.

'And I have seen Warne, staring down the pitch, lips pursed, eyes telling the batsman: "Now I've worked you out. Now I've got you." And the pause at the back of his "run", the panther-stroll to the wicket and contortion of the shoulder, the gasp of pain and effort at the ball's release, and once again the triumph, a thing of which he never tired.

'Warne is like Roger Federer in his ability to produce skills of extraordinary delicacy under extremes of pressure; he is like Tiger Woods in his willingness to go beyond the limits set by the greatest exponents of his art. And so it comes to a close, a decade and a half in which he imposed his will, a decade and a half in which he never once surprised. But always amazed.'

Performance qualities of Shane Warne are listed below.

- An example of **technical** quality is 'Warne is like Roger Federer in his ability to produce skills of extraordinary delicacy under extremes of pressure'.

- An example of **physical** quality is 'In times of trouble, in times of strength, these were the men who stepped forward'.

- An example of **personal** quality is 'thrived on responsibility'.

- An example of **special** quality is '… you remember the command. The command of space and time; each player's certainty that the moment belonged to him'.

KEY CONCEPT 3: MENTAL FACTORS INFLUENCING PERFORMANCE

The management of emotions is very important at all levels of performance. Thus, this key concept concentrates on the mental factors that influence performance and examines different methods of improving the management of your emotions before and during performance.

Mental factors affecting performance include:

- Motivation
- Confidence
- Concentration.

You can read about these factors in detail on pages 72 to 74.

Mental fitness is also an important feature of Area 2 Preparation of the Body, and you will find information about this in Chapter 4. On page 50, mental fitness training methods are detailed. If you possess these performance qualities it enables you to work **at the limit** of your potential, to keep setting new performance targets and avoid complacency based on performing within your **comfort zone**.

TASK

Comfort zone: *Tennis*

Your comfort zone is defined by your **expectations** about how well you are going to perform. If your expectation is that against a known opponent you will probably be beaten by about 6 games to 3, then if you find yourself in a winning position e.g. taking a 5 games to 1 lead you may find yourself getting anxious. This is because you are achieving more than you expected; you are outside your comfort zone. Your increased anxiety might lead to you playing defensively, worrying about losing your lead and trying to 'sit' on your lead. In such a situation it would be better to raise your expectations so that you only become comfortable when achieving better results: in this example by winning the tennis set.

LET'S THINK ABOUT THIS

Have you had any performance experiences where your level of expectation was too low? How did this affect your performance?

MANAGING YOUR EMOTIONS

Imagery

Recall

The aim of imagery practice is to use all your senses to recreate or create an experience in your mind. The following points are important for the effective use of imagery:

- Imagery needs to be practised but it can be of great benefit to your performance.

contd

MANAGING YOUR EMOTIONS contd

- Try to visualise the performance in your imagination in as much detail as you can. Make sure you visualise your whole performance.

- Write it down, keep it and add to it as your actual performance develops and improves.

- Base your imagined performance on positive experiences.

- Use hearing and touch to recreate your imagined performance as well.

Imagery: *High Jump*

Benefits of imagery

- Imagery allows you to slow down and identify the key parts of the high jump.

- It enables you to define your goals before you expect them to occur.

- Successful imagery enables you to turn negative thoughts about what you fear might happen into positive thoughts about what you want to happen.

Imagery: *Rugby – drop kick*

- Hold the ball in front of you in two hands

- Make sure the ball is in position to be dropped onto the pitch

- Watch ball closely

- As you move forward with your non-kicking foot, lift the ball up a little to waist level

- When you drop the ball bring knee forwards and upwards ready to strike the ball as it bounces on the pitch.

- Keep your body weight forward and over the ball

- Use your arms to maintain balance

- Follow through and step up onto non-kicking foot

RELAXATION TECHNIQUES

- Lie down in a warm, comfortable space with a pillow under your head.

- Close your eyes and breathe deeply through your nose in a steady rhythm for a few minutes.

- Don't let your mind wander – focus and be aware of your breathing throughout.

- Continue breathing like this for a few minutes. When you are finished, lie quietly for a further few minutes with your eyes closed.

- Open your eyes and continue lying quietly for a few minutes longer.

LET'S THINK ABOUT THIS

Try to explain the techniques you have used to develop positive feelings about your performance in the different activities in your course.

DON'T FORGET

Imagery and relaxation techniques help prepare you to achieve your performance goals. Performance anxiety can be managed and your emotions controlled by developing positive feelings and overcoming fears and negative feelings about your performance.

DON'T FORGET

Relaxation and recovery between performances are essential in some sports, e.g. between tennis games. Use relaxation techniques to relieve muscle tension and control your breathing. Combine these with imagery exercises to maximise benefit from the recovery period. Remember that you only need to visualise for a short period to enhance performance.

Recall

Identifying those factors which **help** or **hinder** your performance is a useful starting point. Review how the five factors listed in Table 3.3 might influence performance.

		Help performance	Hinder performance
Anxiety		Some golfers prefer playing competitive golf games as they play better when they have a need to win.	Other golfers can become over anxious when faced with playing certain shots, for example, driving when one side of the fairway is 'out of bounds'.
Self-confidence		A self-confident gymnast will include new and different techniques and movements in their routines.	A gymnast lacking in confidence is unlikely to include new and different techniques and movements in their routines, even though they possess the necessary performance abilities.
Level of arousal		Positive levels of arousal (a feeling of excitement) can help performance.	Negative levels of arousal (a feeling of apprehension) can hinder your performance.
Codes of conduct		Playing according to the formal rules and expectations of fair play benefit performance in football.	Breaking the formal rules and code of conduct associated with fair play in football can hinder and distract from effective performance, for example, if you are deliberately over physical when tackling or dive unnecessarily when being tackled.
Event/competition		Some basketball players enjoy performing on big occasions in front of spectators.	Other basketball players find it stressful to perform in front of spectators.

Table 3.3 Factors influencing performance

LET'S THINK ABOUT THIS

You should now understand how mental preparation techniques can aid your performance and how you can overcome mental factors which hold you back.

KEY CONCEPT 4: THE USE OF APPROPRIATE MODELS OF PERFORMANCE

Basing your training priorities on the performance of a model performer can be very beneficial. The observation checklist below could be used for comparison with a model performer as the criteria defined (left hand side of checklist) indicate what a model performance would look like.

Essential features		Self check 1	Self check 2
Preparation ● Swim towards wall at controlled speed ● Adjust arm action cycle to begin turn at correct point and with preferred lead arm	1		
Action ● Initiate turn as leading arm sweeps across body ● Pull hips forward and forward somersault ● Tuck head in tight ● Place feet on the wall approximately half a metre below water surface ● Push off the wall and twist onto your front (if swimming front crawl) ● Extend arms forward to aid streamlining as you drive from wall	2 / 3		
Recovery ● Keep arms forward to maintain streamline shape during recovery ● Begin leg kick and arm action as you surface	4		

Table 3.3.1 Tumble turn

DON'T FORGET

In this key concept you examine in detail the merits of comparing and contrasting your performance with a model performer and the importance of using different methods for collecting feedback about performance.

Recall

Model performers are not always excellent performers of high ability. They can also be 'higher level' performers, who you can more easily compare your own strengths and weaknesses with. At different stages in your performance development you need to compare and contrast your performance with model performers operating at different levels.

Using appropriate models of performance can provide you with useful information on such issues as fitness needs, preparation, skills and decision-making.

DON'T FORGET

Useful methods for collecting feedback in order to compare your performance with a model performance include:
● knowledge of results
● knowledge of previous performance
● error detection/correction
● personal reflection
● use of video/dictaphone.
See pages 8–14 for further information about these methods of collecting information.

 LET'S THINK ABOUT THIS

What information have you collected by comparing your performance with a model performer in the different activities in your course?

KEY CONCEPT 5: PLANNING AND MANAGING PERSONAL PERFORMANCE IMPROVEMENT

Recall

Some of the different qualities (technical, physical, personal) mentioned earlier (pages 19–21) can be used when evaluating the strengths and weaknesses of an individual, team or group performance.

GOAL-SETTING: NETBALL

- Goal-setting principles could link to the **physical** aspects of fitness e.g. a wing attack in netball requires good strength to secure possession.

- Goal-setting principles could link **technical** aspects of performance e.g. controlling space when defending.

- Goal-setting principles could link to aspects of strategy planning e.g. by considering the **personal** qualities each player in your team possesses.

TYPES OF GOALS

As well as following general principles of goal setting, it is useful to define the main types of goals you wish to achieve. There are three main types of goal: outcome goals; performance goals; and process goals.

Outcome goals focus on the result of a particular competition or event such as a 200 m athletics sprint race. Outcome goals are based on comparing yourself against other performers.

Performance goals focus on individual performance and not on comparing your performance against others. For example, performance goals for a 200 m runner would be geared towards race time improvements rather than competition results against opponents. Achieving performance goals may result in you being satisfied with your performance even though you do not achieve your outcome goals e.g. completing the 200 m in a fast time, but not winning the race.

Process goals focus on technique rather than results e.g. by focusing on the stride pattern and relaxation of the upper body when sprinting in athletics rather than on the time taken to complete races. Performers in sports which require precision, e.g. golf, often benefit from setting process goals.

contd

LET'S THINK ABOUT THIS

Most performers try to set a number of different goals as this avoids the limitations associated with setting outcome goals only. Defining only outcome goals can lead to increasing anxiety if, for example, your team fails to win a football match as expected.

TYPES OF GOALS contd

Types of goals: *Tennis*

Examples of different types for the example of tennis are listed in Table 3.4.

Outcome goal		My aim is to beat my opponent in a best of three sets match.
Performance goal		Our aim overall is to improve our play as a doubles unit during competitive games.
Process goal		My aim is to improve my racket preparation when playing forehand shots.

Table 3.4 Goals in tennis

LET'S THINK ABOUT THIS

What types of goals have you identified for the different activities in your course?

SHORT-TERM AND LONG-TERM GOALS

Recall

When setting goals you need to specify exactly what you want to achieve. Achieving long-term goals should be based on achieving a series of short-term goals. For example, if your long-term goal is to swim in the 100 m back crawl race at the national swim championship for your age group this needs to be preceded by achieving shorter term goals. The relationship between short-term goals and your longer term goal can often be considered as a 'staircase' model of goal setting.

Short-term and long-term goal: *Swimming (100 m back crawl)*

May — Represent region at national event
March — Achieve selection for regional team
January — Win school age group (training 4 days per week)
November — Improving strength and refining technique
September — Off-season training

MANAGING YOUR DEVELOPMENT NEEDS

When monitoring, reviewing and evaluating your overall performance it is useful to set performance goals which are based on your current level of ability. This is because accurate goal setting

- is an effective way of helping you understand your performance targets
- can motivate you towards performance improvement
- can help reduce anxieties you may have about your performance.

When setting goals, it is useful to follow certain principles. The acronym SMARTER is one way of explaining how goal-setting can work for you.

EFFECTIVE GOAL-SETTING

In monitoring, reviewing and evaluating your progress, your performance goals should not be too easy or too difficult – they should reflect your current level of ability.

- Goals should challenge you but not intimidate you.
- Accurate goals will help to define your performance targets.
- Achieving your goals is a powerful motivating force.
- Achieving successive goals reduces anxieties about your abilities to perform at a higher level.

Goals have to be carefully considered and certain guidelines should be followed. The acronym 'SMARTER' is one of the most effective techniques in goal-setting.

THE SMARTER TECHNIQUE

- **Specific:** Your goals should be based on your experience and ability; focus on exactly what you want to improve, e.g. improving your service in tennis not just being a better tennis player.
- **Measurable:** Set an easily measurable improvement target, e.g. running 400 m two seconds faster.
- **Agreed:** Your goals need to be agreed with your teacher or coach. This means that you are not working on your own but have their support and input.
- **Realistic:** Unrealistic goals will not be achieved and your morale will suffer. On the other hand, if your goal is realistic and can be attained, you will continue to be motivated.
- **Time-phased:** Make your goals progressive. You should have short-term and longer-term deadlines. Achieving your short-term goals leads to achieving your longer-term goals.
- **Exciting:** You must be motivated and excited by the continuous improvements in your performance. Don't allow yourself to get bored. Your goals should reflect this. Make them fun and rewarding!
- **Recorded:** Keep good performance records in a training diary. Note milestones of achievement and remember – it should always be kept up-to-date.

LET'S THINK ABOUT THIS

Can you explain the short and long-term goals you have selected for the different activities in your course?

KEY WORDS SUMMARY

Key concepts in Performance Appreciation	Key words
Overall nature and demands of quality performance	experiential, precision, control, accuracy
Technical, physical, personal and special qualities of performance	emotional control, codes of conduct, imagination, flair, creativity
Mental factors influencing performance	motivation, managing stress, self-confidence, comfort zone, visualisation
The use of appropriate models of performance	personal style, mental imagery
Planning and managing personal performance improvement	on-going monitoring of performance, setting performance goals

KEY CONCEPT 1: FITNESS ASSESSMENT IN RELATION TO PERSONAL PERFORMANCE AND THE DEMANDS OF ACTIVITIES

COLLECTING SPECIFIC FITNESS INFORMATION

Recall

Collecting specific data on your overall fitness is an essential first step in a training programme. This way you will get accurate information on your current strengths and weaknesses and how your performance is being affected.

Fitness assessments can be carried out by using fitness tests and also through performance in activities. Used effectively, assessments will provide you with accurate information about your physical, skill-related and mental fitness. They should therefore preferably be standardised tests, reflect the nature of the activity being carried out and be regularly monitored.

Collecting specific fitness information: Hockey

Table 4.1 lists specific fitness information for hockey.

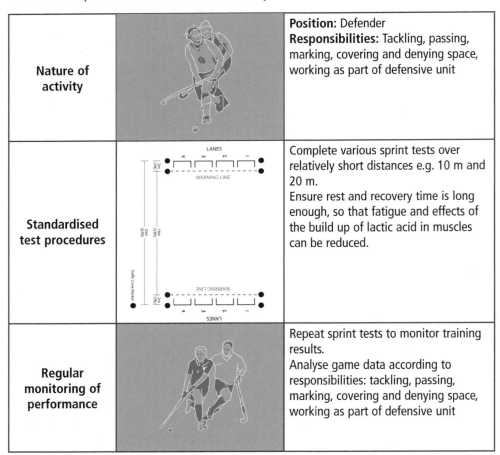

Nature of activity		**Position:** Defender **Responsibilities:** Tackling, passing, marking, covering and denying space, working as part of defensive unit
Standardised test procedures		Complete various sprint tests over relatively short distances e.g. 10 m and 20 m. Ensure rest and recovery time is long enough, so that fatigue and effects of the build up of lactic acid in muscles can be reduced.
Regular monitoring of performance		Repeat sprint tests to monitor training results. Analyse game data according to responsibilities: tackling, passing, marking, covering and denying space, working as part of defensive unit

Table 4.1 Specific fitness information

FITNESS TESTING

Recall

Fitness tests are a simple and easily-administered way to obtain accurate information on your physical fitness level. Using the same fitness assessment at various stages throughout your programme will allow you to accurately measure your progress and development. This is because they are easy to use, do not require complicated equipment and can be self-administered.

The 12-Minute Cooper Test and the Multistage Fitness Test are examples of cardio-respiratory endurance tests.

12-minute Cooper Test

Aim	To calculate your level of cardio-respiratory endurance by applying a time/distance formula
Equipment	A flat area e.g. outdoor field or athletics track
Test procedure	12 minutes to cover the maximum distance possible through running, jogging or walking
Test calculation	Use the table below to measure your own performance.

PERFORMER		PERFORMANCE LEVEL			
age	sex	excellent	good	fair	poor
13-14 years	male	2700	2400	2200	2100
	female	2000	1900	1600	1500
15-16 years	male	2800	2500	2300	2200
	female	2100	1900	1700	1500
17-18 years	male	3000	2700	2500	2300
	female	2300	2100	1800	1500

Multistage Fitness Test

Aim: The aim of the Multistage Fitness Test is to monitor the development of your maximum oxygen uptake.

Equipment: A flat, non-slippery floor surface at least 20 m in length is required. Marking cones and a pre-recorded audio tape or CD and tape recorder or CD player is also required.

Test Procedure: You must place one foot on or beyond the 20 m marker line at the end of each shuttle. You must arrive at the end of a shuttle before the beep and then wait for the beep before resuming running. You keep running for as long as possible until you can no longer keep up with the speed set by the tape. If you fail to reach the end of the shuttle before the beep you are allowed two further shuttles to attempt to regain the required pace before your test finishes. Record the level and number of shuttles completed at that level.

contd

FITNESS TESTING contd

Test Calculation: The test is made up of 23 levels with each level lasting approximately one minute. Each level comprises a series of 20 m shuttles. The starting speed is 8.5 km/hr and increases by 0.5 km/hr at each level. A single beep on the tape indicates the end of a shuttle and 3 beeps indicates the start of the next level. You can then measure your performance against predicted maximum oxygen uptake values (VO_2 Max): see Table 4.2. For example, if you continue running until Level 15 and successfully complete 10 shuttles at this level before your test finishes, then your VO_2 Max figure is 66.7.

Level	Shuttle	VO_2 Max	Level	Shuttle	VO_2 Max	Level	Shuttle	VO_2 Max
6	2	33.6	7	2	37.1	10	2	47.4
6	4	34.3	7	4	37.8	10	4	48.0
6	6	35.0	7	6	38.5	10	6	48.7
6	8	35.7	7	8	39.2	10	8	49.3
6	10	36.4	7	10	39.9	10	10	50.2

Level	Shuttle	VO_2 Max	Level	Shuttle	VO_2 Max	Level	Shuttle	VO_2 Max
14	2	61.1	15	2	64.6	18	2	74.8
14	4	61.7	15	4	65.1	18	4	75.3
14	6	62.2	15	6	65.6	18	6	75.8
14	8	62.7	15	8	66.2	18	8	76.2
14	10	63.2	15	10	66.7	18	10	76.7
14	12	64.0	15	12	67.5	18	12	77.2
						18	15	77.9

Table 4.2 Predicted maximum oxygen uptake levels for running test

OTHER TYPES OF FITNESS TEST

Physical fitness tests exist for other aspects of physical fitness. Consider the examples in Table 4.3.

Aspect of physical fitness		Fitness test	Test procedure
Muscular endurance		The Bent Knee Sit-Up test is an effective test for measuring the muscular endurance of the abdominal (stomach) muscles.	Lie flat on floor. A full sit-up is counted when you curl your back, raise your trunk until your lower back is at least 90 degrees to the floor. Repeat for time interval e.g. 60 seconds. A partner can provide resistance by holding ankles.
Strength (dynamic)		Press up or inclined press up test is an effective test for measuring dynamic strength.	Ensure your body and legs are in a straight line, with your arms extended and at an angle of 90 degrees to the body.
Speed		Timed sprint test over 20 m is an effective test for measuring speed.	Ensure distances are accurately measured and that time-keeping procedures are clear.

Power		The Standing Long Jump test is an effective test for measuring the power (explosive strength) of the leg muscles.	Complete a two-footed jump and measure the distance from the marked start line to the back of your furthest back foot on landing.
Flexibility		The Trunk Extension test is an effective test for measuring the flexibility of the lower back.	With your hands grasped behind your neck, gradually raise your upper trunk from the ground and hold for three seconds. Repeat.

Table 4.3 Fitness tests and procedures

LET'S THINK ABOUT THIS

What physical fitness tests have you completed in your course?

SKILL-RELATED FITNESS TESTS

Fitness tests exist for various aspects of skill-related fitness as well. Consider the examples in Table 4.4.

Aspect of skill-related fitness		Fitness test	Test procedure	Fitness rating		
Agility		The Illinois Agility Run test combines running with many different changes of direction and is a recognised test for agility.	Start lying prone on ground. On the start signal run the course shown as quickly as possible. Record your time and fitness rating.	**TIME IN SECONDS**		**RATING**
				males	*females*	
				<15.2	<17.0	excellent
				16.1 - 15.2	17.9 - 17.0	good
				18.1 - 16.2	21.7 - 18.0	average
				18.3 - 18.2	23.0 - 21.8	fair
				>18.3	>23.0	poor
Balance		Balancing on a beam is an effective test for measuring static balance.	Time how long you can remain in balance on one foot with eyes closed on a balance beam or inverted bench.	Timed in seconds. Class comparisons possible.		
Coordination		Learning to juggle is a possible measurement of coordination	Time how long it takes to learn to juggle three tennis balls.	Timed in minutes. Class comparisons possible.		
Reaction time		The Stick Drop test is an effective test for measuring reaction time.	Partner holds ruler. You place your chosen hand on the 50cm mark of the ruler. Without warning, your partner drops the ruler and you must catch it between thumb and index finger as soon as possible. Record your best result from three attempts.	*reaction time*		*rate*
				>42.5		excellent
				34.1 - 42.5		good
				29.6 - 37.0		average
				22.0 - 29.5		fair
				<22		poor

Table 4.4 Skill-related fitness tests

FITNESS INFORMATION FROM WHOLE PERFORMANCE

Recall

Very often, you will use your whole performance for collecting relevant fitness information. This can be a useful method of assessing different types of fitness as results reflect your practical ability, your role within an activity and your individual and team goals.

Example: *Football game*

One method of collecting cardio-respiratory information from a football game is to measure your pulse throughout the game. Data from a heart rate monitor can be transferred to a computer and displayed as a graph for analysis of your fitness.

The evidence from this graph indicates that the performer was able to maintain a high level of physical involvement throughout the game. However, gradually they became more tired as the game progressed. This is evident by the lower average pulse for the second half (150) as opposed to the first half (155) and the sharper peaks and troughs shown in the pulse readings. These indicate that sprint-type runs in the second half began to tire the player and it took longer for them to recover than in the first half of the match.

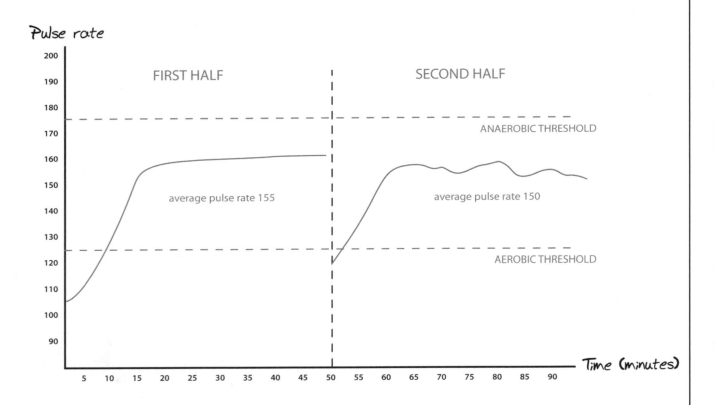

⚙ LET'S THINK ABOUT THIS

When during your course have you collected fitness-related information from your whole performance?

contd

FITNESS INFORMATION FROM WHOLE PERFORMANCE contd

Example: *Gymnastics*

It is often beneficial to use both fitness tests and your whole performance to collect information. In this way the results of your fitness tests can be considered alongside your whole performance findings. For example, to measure your degree of flexibility in gymnastics, you could use the following methods for gathering information.

1. **Whole performance (gymnastics routine):** Complete your gymnastics floor sequence. Rest for five minutes. Repeat on two further occasions. Record in your training diary the movements in your routine which require most flexibility. Note the major joint around which flexibility in muscles is required. Record in your training diary whether lack of flexibility limits your performance.

2. **Fitness tests:** Complete set of five flexibility exercises working with a partner. (See suitable exercises on page 49.) Rest for two minutes. Repeat a further three times. Partner to add degree of resistance as appropriate.

The fitness tests would provide objective information to support any conclusions you may be able to draw from your whole performance results. If your gymnastics routine had improved in qualitative terms this might be because your flexibility had improved. By contrast, it could be that if your gymnastics routine did not improve but your flexibility results were better. These findings would imply that other factors e.g. your gymnastics technique had influenced the quality of your performance.

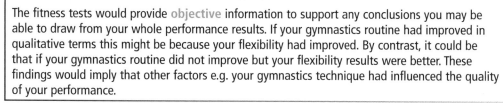

LET'S THINK ABOUT THIS

Can you explain the fitness assessment procedures you have followed on your course?

LET'S THINK ABOUT THIS

You should try to explain how the various activities on your course were informed by the relevant and accurate fitness information you have collected.

MENTAL FITNESS

Recall

Relevant assessments about how mental fitness influences performance can be gathered effectively from whole performance situations. For example, a basketball team may regularly concede late points due to fatigue and loss of focus. Knowing that this was the cause of the drop-off in performance, a training programme should be geared towards improving team concentration and focus throughout the whole game.

There tend to be fewer objective-based tests to measure mental fitness. This is because mental fitness is much more subjective and more difficult to measure precisely than objective-based fitness assessments. Instead, there are strategies for identifying key mental fitness issues.

Self-talk

One strategy for identifying mental fitness issues is to develop your self-talk abilities. Positive self-talk, where you think and talk about issues which are central to improving performance, is useful for reminding you of the essential fitness and skill requirements as well as the necessary flow and feeling of movements.

For further information about mental factors which influence performance, see pages 41–42.

KEY CONCEPT 2: APPLICATION OF DIFFERENT TYPES OF FITNESS IN THE DEVELOPMENT OF ACTIVITY SPECIFIC PERFORMANCE

Recall

When considering improving your fitness in relation to activity-specific performance it is important that you

- set specific performance goals
- analyse the nature and demands of the activity
- analyse your own particular role within the activity.

This will enable you to create a targeted training programme that reflects your abilities.

DEVELOPING PHYSICAL FITNESS

It is important to select the correct training method for your own needs, whether it is in the activity or outwith the activity.

Both types of training can be helpful provided you complete them properly. You can also combine the two methods.

Training through activities (conditioning)

DEVELOPING SKILL-RELATED FITNESS

The two approaches highlighted above for developing physical fitness could also apply to skill-related fitness.

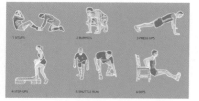

- **Conditioning approach to fitness training:** In games such as netball, hockey, football and rugby, you could organise conditioned games or practices to develop skills as well as fitness. For example, both your fitness and skills can be developed through practice games of lengthening duration and against opposing teams of better, more skilful, players.
- **Fitness training outside of activities:** Alternatively, you could also improve your skill and fitness through a skill-related fitness training programme outside or away from the activity, such as circuit training.

Training outside of activities

DEVELOPING MENTAL ASPECTS OF FITNESS

Actual match practice and regular competition against skilled opposition are both vital in developing mental fitness, for example, competitiveness, concentration and emotional control.

Imagining situations and moves is a critical part of mental preparation in many sports. For example a slalom kayaker should mentally visualise their progress down the river and imagine what precisely they will do to get the best lines and fastest movements.

LET'S THINK ABOUT THIS

You should be able to explain the information you considered when setting specific performance objectives.

KEY CONCEPT 3: PHYSICAL, SKILL-RELATED AND MENTAL TYPES OF FITNESS

RELATIONSHIPS BETWEEN DIFFERENT ASPECTS OF FITNESS

To be successful in an activity you need a mixture of different types of physical, skill-related and mental aspects of fitness.

Relationships between different aspects of fitness: *High jump*

To perform the high jump in athletics you require power (an aspect of physical fitness), coordination (an aspect of skill-related fitness) and imagery (an aspect of mental fitness). When the drive is initiated, considerable power is necessary in the legs and arms of the jumper to generate height. As the drive occurs, ensuring that the back begins to arch as the hips gain height in a coordinated way is also required. To perform such a complex technique in a short space of time benefits from imagery about the key parts of the high jump. Successful imagery enables you to have positive thoughts about what you want to happen.

DON'T FORGET

For this key concept, you should be familiar with aspects of fitness, how they interrelate and in what ways each aspect can be worked into a training programme.

LET'S THINK ABOUT THIS

Choose one skill or technique that you have worked on during your course and describe how different aspects of physical, skill-related and mental fitness are required for effective performance.

ASPECTS OF PHYSICAL FITNESS

Recall

- **Cardiorespiratory endurance** is the ability of the whole body to work continuously.

- **Muscular endurance** is the ability of the muscles to work continuously.

- **Strength** is the maximum amount of force a muscle, or group of muscles, can exert in a single effort.

- **Speed** is the ability to cover a distance or perform a movement in a short time.

- **Power** is the combination of strength and speed.

- **Flexibility** is the range of movement across a joint.

LINKS BETWEEN DIFFERENT ASPECTS OF PHYSICAL FITNESS

Different aspects of physical fitness are often linked together when performance improvement is planned.

Speed endurance

In tennis, you need to develop both cardio-respiratory endurance and speed. These may appear initially as quite independent aspects of physical fitness. However, to improve both, it is often best to link them together. This could result in designing a training programme which links a general base of cardio-respiratory work with shorter bursts of speed work, leading to the overall development of speed endurance. Your training will benefit you when playing long competitive games of tennis where speed for fast, intermittent bursts of play around the court is required throughout the game.

Strength endurance

In hockey, slap hitting the ball involves major muscle groups working together to produce a strong action which can be repeated, if necessary, throughout a long hockey match. This requires both muscular endurance and strength.

 LET'S THINK ABOUT THIS

Try to describe any activities on your course where speed endurance or strength endurance is required.

DIFFERENCES WITHIN CERTAIN ASPECTS OF PHYSICAL FITNESS

 DON'T FORGET

As well as links between different aspects of physical fitness there are also differences within certain aspects of physical fitness.

Strength examples

There are three main types of strength. There is static strength, explosive strength and dynamic strength.

- **Static strength:** Players in a rugby scrum resist the pressure of opposing players in order to hold their position and not let their opponents drive them backwards. Players in a scrum require static strength.

- **Explosive strength:** Performers use explosive strength when they need to carry out one fast movement with the maximum amount of force. Examples could be long jump or discus throw.

- **Dynamic strength:** Dynamic strength is required in events such as cycling, swimming and sprinting that take up to approximately two minutes. For example, in the 200m race a sprinter continuously uses the major muscles of the arm and shoulder to generate speed.

In longer events, such as the 1500m, fatigue sets in and athletes need local muscular endurance more than dynamic strength. Fatigue is caused by a build-up of waste products in the muscle cells as the athlete tries to keep going over a more prolonged period.

contd

DIFFERENCES WITHIN CERTAIN ASPECTS OF PHYSICAL FITNESS contd

It is very important to remember that, in athletics, swimming and cycling, you will require different training programmes for improving your dynamic strength and improving your muscular endurance.

Flexibility examples

There are two types of flexibility: static and dynamic flexibility. Static flexibility is necessary when you are holding a balance in gymnastics. Dynamic flexibility requires flexibility for a short time within your overall performance. For example, a high jumper requires dynamic flexibility when arching their back during the jump.

LET'S THINK ABOUT THIS

Are you able to explain two aspects of physical fitness which were required for an activity in your course?

ASPECTS OF SKILL-RELATED FITNESS

Recall

Agility

Agility can be defined as the capacity to move the body quickly, flexibly and precisely. An example of an activity requiring agility is dribbling in football, where speedy balanced movements must be combined with ball control. Agility is also required in such disparate activities as rock climbing and dance.

Reaction time

Reaction time can be defined as the time that elapses between the recognition of a stimulus and the start of the response. In a sprint race, reaction time is the time between the starting signal and the first movement of the sprinter. Performers with quick reaction times have advantages over other performers. For example, in cricket the time available to decide whether to move forward or back to play the ball is often as little as 0.3 seconds when a fast bowler is bowling.

As your reaction time improves, you are likely to think and respond more quickly. This should lead to fewer errors in movement and more time to make appropriate decisions. For example, in a lineout in rugby union, practice between the thrower and the jumpers and other players in your team involved should ensure that your team are able to secure possession. This will be more difficult to achieve when the opposing team have the throw in, as you will have less time to respond and time your jump accordingly.

> **DON'T FORGET**
>
> There are several aspects of skill related fitness that you should remember! Agility, balance, coordination, movement anticipation, reaction time and timing all apply so try to form a system to make sure you keep them in mind.

> **DON'T FORGET**
>
> Try not to mistake aspects of skill-related fitness with Skills and Techniques when answering Analysis and Development of Performance questions.

contd

LET'S THINK ABOUT THIS

Reaction times can be improved by detecting relevant cues e.g. when goalkeeping in football try to analyse the body language of the penalty taker and make movement decisions on such evidence.

Balance

Balance can be defined as being able to hold the centre of weight or centre of gravity over the base of support. Balance is maintained by different muscle groups which vary depending on the activity or movement being carried out.

Static balance: A headstand in gymnastics requires you to hold a static balance. As your static balance improves, you are more likely to be able to show greater control of your strength and body weight. In the headstand balance, you move from using large body movements to completing the balance by using small body movements. This improves your stability and indicates a good sense of balance.

Dynamic balance: A white water kayaker has to maintain dynamic balance under rapidly changing conditions. As their dynamic balance improves they are more likely to be able to remain in control in more demanding situations..

Balance can sometimes be improved by lowering your centre of gravity and widening the base of support. For example, in volleyball you are more likely to play a good 'dig' shot if you have a secure balance based on having a low centre of gravity and wide base of support.

By contrast, the greater movement required to play a service return in tennis means that many players deliberately stand tall with a narrow base of support just as the serve is played. This makes it easier for them to move quickly to the side as soon as possible to try to return the serve.

Timing

Timing can be defined as the ability to choose exactly the correct moment to execute a movement or action to achieve maximum impact. Timing involves different skills in different activities. For example, in tennis or badminton it is necessary to judge where the ball or shuttle will be when the racquet makes contact. In golf, strength must be carefully controlled to maximise the effectiveness of the swing.

Coordination

Coordination can be defined as the capacity to execute movements in a fluid and effortless manner. The more complex the task, the greater the level of coordination required. As your coordination improves, you are able to move your joints and muscles in the correct order. This leads to improvements in for example, your hand and eye coordination, which is important in activities where striking or hitting actions are required. To complete a slap hit in hockey you require coordination in addition to strength endurance to ensure that your strength endurance is used at the correct stage of the slap hit.

Movement anticipation

Movement anticipation can be defined as the ability to predict how you are going to respond to your opponent. In volleyball, you require movement anticipation to respond and move quickly in order to get behind the ball as much as possible. Thereafter, you can use your secure balance (created by low centre of gravity and wide base of support) to play an effective dig shot. In this example, movement anticipation would be improved by watching your opponents play carefully and anticipating as early as possible the direction of their next shot and moving accordingly.

DON'T FORGET

Just as there are often links between different aspects of physical fitness, so there are links between different aspects of skill-related fitness e.g. a skier requires not only dynamic balance to maintain balance under constantly changing conditions but also agility in order to move the body quickly and precisely.

⚙ LET'S THINK ABOUT THIS

Which two aspects of skill-related fitness have been most useful to you during your course? Explain their usefulness for two activities in your course.

ASPECTS OF MENTAL FITNESS

Recall

Level of arousal

Your level of arousal must be optimal for best performance. Over-excitement and/or stress and anxiety caused by high expectations for your performance (high arousal) can be just as damaging as fatigue, disinterest or complacency (low arousal).

Levels of arousal vary between performers and between activities. For complex skills in competitive situations, a low level of arousal is usually required e.g. when putting in golf. By contrast, simple routine tasks when training often require a higher level of arousal. If your level of arousal is not at the optimum level it can often be increased by an active warm up, music or a motivational speech. Relaxation techniques or soothing music can be used when you are over-aroused before performance.

> **DON'T FORGET**
>
> There are several aspects of mental fitness that you should remember! Level of arousal, rehearsal and managing emotions all apply so try to form a system to make sure you keep them in mind.

Rehearsal

Rehearsal is taking a momentary break before a performance to conjure up a mental picture of what you want your performance to look like. By rehearsing in your mind what is about to occur, the intention is that you can replace any negative thoughts with positive thoughts. This will help increase your confidence and establish a feeling of flow. The imagery-based examples on pages 22–23 are examples of where mental rehearsal is expected to help performance improvement.

Flow: *Rugby*

In a rugby union team there is much more than physical fitness intensity required. A good team works seamlessly together; as a move by the quicker backs breaks down, the forwards move in as fast as possible to the scene of the breakdown, maul and ruck for the ball and set up the next attacking phase. The play flows as each player understands their role within the team. The team that can find the pace and flow required to bring about coherent phases of play will often win the game.

Flow: *Golf*

In golf, rehearsal often involves trying to recognise where the basis for a good swing comes from. Focus on small details such as the golf club grip, but also consider how the feeling or flow of large parts of the body, such as the stomach and shoulders, contribute to an effective golf swing.

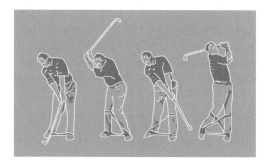

contd

Managing your emotions

Both individuals and teams need to have a mentally disciplined approach to situations that can arise during a game. For example, this can involve screening out distraction when taking a penalty in football or rugby. Having a clear and focused mind will bring out the best performance.

The emotions within a team can also be important. A committed and disciplined team will show determination and team resolve to get on even terms after losing a goal.

Links between different aspects of mental fitness

Just as there are often links between different aspects of physical and skill-related fitness, there are links between different aspects of mental fitness. For example, a guard in basketball requires not only the appropriate level of arousal but an ability to manage emotions when defending if they are to help their team defend effectively. If they lack interest in defending (low level of arousal) or are easily distracted (lack of managing emotion) this will have a detrimental effect on performance.

LET'S THINK ABOUT THIS

Which two aspects of mental fitness have been most useful to you during your course? Explain their usefulness to two activities in your course.

Inter-relationship between different aspects of fitness (physical, skill-related and mental): *Netball*

In netball, the centre is the only one of the seven players in a team who moves around the entire court except for the goal circles. Accordingly, the centre has a crucial role in linking defence to attack and vice versa. A good centre will possess a mix of speed endurance, movement anticipation and a moderate level of arousal.

Speed endurance is required because of the combined need to move around most of the entire court for long periods of the game as well as making fast, intermittent sprints at selected times throughout the game. Movement anticipation is necessary so that when you are defending you can respond and move quickly in order to stay between your opposing centre and your own net. This requires watching your opponent carefully and anticipating as early as possible the direction of their movements. In attack, the roles are reversed as you try and use your understanding with your team mates to create space and link forward passes together.

A moderate level of arousal is required. If your level of arousal is too high, you may become anxious or stressed because of the expectations on you to perform well. This might be noticeable in the number of simple passing errors which you make or by the overambitious nature of some of the passes attempted. By contrast, if you are inadequately focused on performance, your low level of arousal might result in sloppy and unnecessarily careless play.

LET'S THINK ABOUT THIS

Can you explain how, for effective performance in the activities in your course, a mixture of physical, skill-related and mental fitness is required?

KEY CONCEPT 4: PRINCIPLES AND METHODS OF TRAINING

PRINCIPLES OF TRAINING

Specificity

For training to be specific it needs to:

- suit your particular needs and requirements
- relate to your own level of fitness and skill
- be relevant to the activity you want to work on
- relate to the energy system (aerobic or anaerobic) which you are trying to improve.

You need to ensure you apply the principle of specificity whether training is completed through a physical fitness or conditioning training programme.

LET'S THINK ABOUT THIS

Try to explain how you ensured that your training was specific to your level of fitness and skill and relevant to the different activities in your course.

Progressive overload

As you exercise at increasingly demanding levels it becomes necessary to apply the training principle of progressive overload to your fitness programme. As your fitness levels improves you create new targets to ensure progressive overload is included in your training. When adding progressive overload and working out new training programme details, the general rule is that making very small increases is ineffective, making moderate increases is useful and making excessive increases is harmful and might well result in unsafe training.

LET'S THINK ABOUT THIS

You should be able to explain how you ensured that progressive overload was added to your training programmes in your course.

Frequency

Frequency relates to how often you train. This will vary according to the demands of the activity. As a general indicator of training frequency, the average performer trying to improve cardiorespiratory (aerobic) endurance would need to exercise with their heart rate in their training zone for 20 to 30 minutes for four or more sessions per week over a two-to-three month period. However, a high level performer in competitive running would often run more frequently. By contrast, if you had just started playing full games of basketball, you would not have to train so often to see an improvement in your fitness.

Improving strength, power and speed (i.e. anaerobic fitness) requires less frequent training. Table 4.5 overleaf contrasts the frequency training demands for swimmers who are trying to improve aerobic and anaerobic fitness.

contd

PRINCIPLES OF TRAINING contd

Training details	Endurance training (aerobic)	Strength/speed training (anaerobic)
Frequency	4–7 sessions per week	3–5 sessions per week
Intensity	Heart rate: 60–85% of maximal heart rate	Heart rate: 85–100% of maximal heart rate
Duration	3–4 months	2.5–3 months

Table 4.5 Frequency training demands: swimming

Intensity

Intensity relates to how challenging your training sessions are. As you progress through your training programme the intensity of your training should increase as you apply the principle of progressive overload. The initial intensity of your training varies according to your pre-test levels of fitness, your longer-term training goals and the demands of different activities.

In order to get the full benefit from aerobic endurance training you need to check your pulse to make sure you are training within your heart rate training zone.

When speed training you need to work at a high level of intensity for shorter periods to improve anaerobic fitness. Through anaerobic training you will improve your body's ability to cope with lactic acid build-up, caused when you use anaerobic respiration to provide energy. Anaerobic exercise can only be sustained for a short period of time as this type of exercise places a great strain on your circulatory and respiratory systems. For these reasons, you need to be aerobically fit before beginning anaerobic endurance training and understand the link between your maximum oxygen uptake and lactic acid threshold. This is because oxygen debt leads to a high level of lactic acid build-up, with the result that your muscles tire, become fatigued and begin to work less effectively. Performers with the ability to tolerate high levels of lactic acid in their muscles are most likely to perform well in activities which demand high levels of local muscular endurance such as swimming and cycling.

You can increase intensity by making your training ever more demanding (i.e. by increasing intensity levels). For example, in training for a 400 m race, you could benefit from a series of sprints carried out at your maximum 100% speed when you need to sprint at 80% of your maximum in the race itself. In applying progressive overload, especially in regard to speed/ strength/power training, make sure that you set the correct intensity levels.

By changing the work/rest interval you can also increase (or reduce) the levels of intensity of your training programme. For example, when following a cardio-respiratory endurance training programme, you could gradually reduce your rest periods, thus increasing the levels of intensity.

Duration

Duration relates to the amount of time that you allocate to your training programmes and to individual training sessions. This will of course depend on the type of activity involved.

Anaerobic fitness:

- short, intensive training sessions
- six to eight weeks at high intensity.

Aerobic fitness:

- longer, moderately intensive training sessions
- two to three months at least four times per week.

Sessions will vary in duration as you progress, for example you might start with 40 minute sessions at the start of your training programme and build up to 60 minutes.

LET'S THINK ABOUT THIS

Try to explain how you developed training programmes for your course activities by adapting the frequency, intensity and duration of your training.

contd

PRINCIPLES OF TRAINING contd

The dangers of over-training

Over-training can occur in all forms of training programme, but its adverse effects can be avoided by ensuring that adequate rest and recovery time is taken between training sessions. Over-training is often caused by trying to do too much too soon. Over-training is often referred to as 'burn out'. The symptoms of over-training are both physiological (decreased capacity for maximum oxygen uptake) as well as psychological (feeling run down, loss of motivation, irritability).

Adequate rest and recovery time is often underestimated. For example, a sprinter needs approximately 5 minutes rest and recovery time between each set of 3 × 200 m sprints. Any less time would result in over-exertion and muscle fatigue, leading to pain and stiffness. An athlete's pulse must return to a normal resting level before starting the next set.

You can reduce the effects of over-training by adjusting the levels of frequency, intensity and duration in your training programme. It is important to consider these three factors when reviewing the effectiveness of your training. A training diary is a useful tool in helping you to analyse how levels of frequency, intensity and duration could be changed to avoid over-training.

⚙ LET'S THINK ABOUT THIS

Can you explain how you ensured that the dangers of over-training were avoided during your course activities?

Reversibility

The benefits gained from training are reversible, i.e. once training finishes, the body reverts to its original condition. The time it takes to lose the beneficial training effects depends on how long you have been training for.

- If you have been training for a short time, for example a few weeks, you will lose the beneficial training effects within a similar time period.

- If you have been training for months, the training benefits will last longer. The reason for this is because, although the body takes a long time to adapt to fitness, once fitness is established it takes a longer time before reversibility occurs.

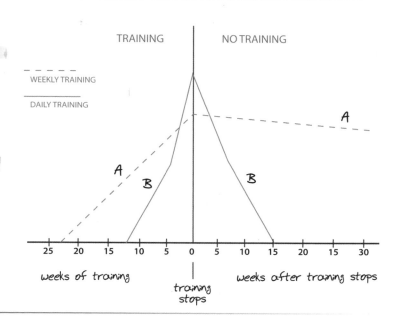

⚙ LET'S THINK ABOUT THIS

Can you explain how the adverse effects of reversibility were avoided while training for your course activities?

METHODS OF TRAINING

Physical fitness training methods

The most important methods of training for physical fitness you should revise are: continuous training, fartlek training, interval training, circuit training, weight training, plyometric and flexibility fitness training.

Continuous training

- **Examples**: running, swimming, cycling or game situations where less than full effort is required and where the heart rate will be in your training zone for approximately 20–30 minutes, three to four times per week.

- **This type of exercise** can benefit your aerobic system by accumulating little lactic acid and allowing you to recover quickly after exercise.

- **The benefits** of continuous training are that it can improve cardio-respiratory endurance and raise the anaerobic threshold. It is relatively easy to plan and progressive overload can be achieved by increasing frequency (exercising more often), increasing intensity (exercising faster) or increasing duration (training for longer).

Fartlek training

- **Examples**: continuous running or swimming where short intense sprints are followed by an easier recovery period and thereafter by more continuous paced running or swimming.

- **This type of exercise** improves both aerobic fitness (continuous running or swimming) by keeping within the training zone and anaerobic fitness (short speed endurance sprints).

- **The benefits** of fartlek training are that it is very flexible and can be adapted to suit individual requirements. For example, different kinds of terrain can be used such as short hills or flat moorland to vary the pace and demands of the run. Progressive overload can be achieved by increasing frequency (exercising more often), increasing intensity (exercising faster) or increasing duration (training for longer).

Interval fitness training

- **Examples**: any form of exercise, e.g. walking, jogging, swimming or cycling during which you can easily calculate a work/rest interval. If this cannot easily be calculated for your chosen activity, you may find it difficult to get the training benefits.

- **This type of exercise** allows high-intensity effort to be undertaken while lowering overall fatigue. For example, a running training programme for a 3000 m runner could include 4 × 800 m repetitions, each lasting 130–140 s with 120 s recovery between each repetition. Fatigue caused by interval training of this sort would be less than that caused by a single 3000 m run. Cardiorespiratory endurance involving running should be calculated on the basis of training at 50–60% of your fastest time. By contrast, speed work would be calculated on 80% of your fastest time.

- **The benefits** of interval fitness training are that it can increase both aerobic and anaerobic capacity. Progressive overload can be achieved by increasing frequency (completing the activity more often), increasing intensity (exercising faster or decreasing rest intervals) or increasing duration (training for longer).

There are three main types of interval training. These are long interval, intermediate interval and short interval training.

Long interval training:

This type of interval training is frequently used by performers requiring high levels of aerobic endurance e.g. athletes completing middle distance running events. Training programmes are based around aerobic and lactic acid tolerance training intervals. Table 4.6 outlines the type of interval training an athlete might complete on a 400 m athletics track.

contd

METHODS OF TRAINING contd

Warm up		
Set 1: 2 × 400 m (1 lap) easy pace running. Time 80–90 seconds		2–3 minute jog recovery after each 400 m run
Set 2: 2 × 800 m (2 laps) easy pace running. Time 2 m 30 secs–3 minutes		5 minute jog recovery after 800 m run
Set 3: 2 × 400 m (1 lap) easy pace running. Time 80–90 seconds		2–3 minute jog recovery after each 400 m run
Warm down		

Table 4.6 Athletics training

Intermediate interval training:

Intermediate interval training is frequently used by games players in outdoor games where the large size of the pitch means that there is little time for rest. Training programmes are based around improving the lactic acid energy system. As this type of training is likely to result in some muscle soreness, it is necessary for adequate recovery time between training intervals.

On outside games pitches you could, for example, run a triangular course based on jogging for 30 m then running for 40 m at 50% of your fastest speed, then running for 50 m at 75% of your fastest speed. After returning to the start point, you could return to jogging to allow you time to recover. As your training progresses, the running distances covered at speed will lead to improvements in your cardio-respiratory endurance and speed.

Short interval training:

Short interval training is used by games players who particularly require sprint speed, for example, a winger in rugby union. Training is adapted for such performers by increasing the intensity of running and also increasing rest intervals. Training could take place in similar ways to that described for the intermediate interval training example above. However, for best results, it would help if the running distances were reduced combined with an increase in the speed of some parts of the running.

Circuit training

- **Examples:** fixed-load circuits, where you complete the same circuit exercises with the same number of exercise repetitions; individual-load circuits where everyone completes a circuit of exercises based on their individual strength and weaknesses (based on pre-exercise testing); and fixed-time circuits where you complete different exercises for a set time interval, e.g. one minute and then everyone moves to the next station. It can also include multi-station circuits.

- **This type of exercise** enables general exercises for different major muscle areas to be combined into an organised circuit as well as specific circuits of exercise which focus on particular areas of fitness development.

- **The benefits** of circuit training are that it improves both general and specific fitness and that exercises can be chosen on a sport-related basis as well as tailored to individual's fitness requirements. In addition, progressive overload can be achieved through increasing frequency (increasing repetitions of exercises).

contd

Weight training

- **Examples:** Isotonic and isometric exercises. You can use free-standing weights and weight machines for both types of exercise. In isotonic exercises the resistance force (the weight) is moved through the range of motion, contracting and lengthening the muscle e.g. when performing a biceps curl. In weight training, isotonic exercises are the most common. In isometric exercises you provide resistance against the weight e.g. in isometric shoulder raises where you raise the weight out to your side until it is at shoulder height and your outstretched arms are parallel to the ground, and then hold the weight steady. Isotonic exercises develop dynamic strength; isometric exercises develop static strength.

- **This type of exercise** enables resistance training to occur based on performing repetitions of set exercises, e.g. 3 sets of 15 repetitions of a bench press. For best results and safe practice, exercises should be arranged so that the same muscle groups are not exercised at successive stations. It is better to complete a weight exercise for the legs after completing an upper body exercise, for example.

- **The benefits** of weight training are that it develops both general and specific muscles and improves muscular endurance, strength and power. You can also easily work out personal values for exercises (e.g. 80–90% of your maximum single lift if based on sets and repetitions for strength). Progressive overload can also be achieved through increasing intensity (increasing weight) or by increasing frequency (increasing repetitions of exercises).

Plyometric training

Plyometrics is a relatively new form of training designed to improve power. Players rebounding in basketball and spiking in volleyball might use plyometrics. Training is based on the idea that standing tall and then bending down before a strong forceful jump is more effective than starting from an already low bent leg position.

- **Includes** bounding type exercises which progress from low to high intensity as coordination and power improve.

- **This type of exercise** is based on powerful contractions (absorptions) by groups of muscles and the idea is that if muscles are pre-stretched before contraction then they can contract more flexibly.

- **The benefits** of plyometric training is that it improves muscular power. Progressive overload is achieved by increasing repetition (frequency).

DON'T FORGET

Safety precautions: Before beginning plyometric training, you require a good level of general conditioning. You must adopt good technique when completing bounding type exercises, so that you do not put excessive strain on muscles, tendons, ligaments and joints. Avoid over-training and ensure that you allow adequate time for rest and recovery.

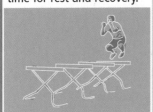

contd

METHODS OF TRAINING contd

Flexibility training

- **Examples:** dynamic or static stretching or resistance exercises. It is important you do not overstretch. Follow correct techniques and always work within your range of movement.

- **This type of exercise** enables you to alternate between major joint and muscle areas as well as completing flexibility exercises which focus on specific areas of fitness development.

- **The benefits** of flexibility training are that it improves your ability to move slowly into stretches. Increasing a range of movement around the joint can be achieved either by holding the end of stretch position for a few seconds or by actively contracting muscles against resistance from a partner. Progressive overload is achieved by increasing frequency (completing the programme more often), increasing intensity (introducing more challenging stretching exercises) or by increasing duration (training for longer).

Static passive stretching and exercises against a degree of resistance: There are a number of flexibility exercises you can complete on your own as part of a static stretching programme, or by exercising against a degree of resistance provided by a partner.

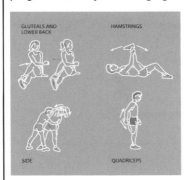

For any of the static passive exercises alongside, ensure that you avoid bouncing or moving quickly into a stretched position.

Pictured alongside are a number of flexibility exercises you can complete either on your own or by working with a partner who can provide a degree of resistance as you contract the muscles.

SKILL-RELATED FITNESS TRAINING METHODS

Football example

- Passing over long distances and running in between passes would be beneficial for improving aerobic exercise and timing, as this is important in long passing.

- Screening and tackling practices would be beneficial for improving reaction time and movement anticipation.

- Dribbling practices would be useful for improving agility as both speed and coordination are required in the practice.

- Passing over shorter distances with more frequent changes of movement would be good for improving balance; staying in dynamic balance is important when passing, moving and turning.

DON'T FORGET

A popular method of skill-related fitness training involves team members following a circuit of different skill-related practices. The football example opposite highlights practices which have both physical and skill-related fitness demands.

MENTAL FITNESS TRAINING METHODS

The most important strategies for training for mental fitness are listed below.

DON'T FORGET

It is worth investigating the various different types of mental training which will help you manage your emotions better during performance. Different activities demand different approaches, hence the variety.

- When practising imagery before a performance, find a quiet spot where you won't be disturbed.

- Make sure you visualise your best possible performance.

- Try to avoid negative perceptions about performance, as this will lead to increased anxiety.

- Recognise that you can control what you are thinking about and direct your thoughts towards more productive and positive perceptions about performance.

- Build on your positive perception of performance by recording positive achievements in a journal or diary.

- Consider including centring techniques into your preparation. Centring involves breathing deeply and slowly and focusing on your abdomen. By focusing on your abdomen (centre of gravity), you can often increase your feeling of control and balance and consequently become better placed to focus on positive performance.

- Think about the most important aspects of performance. For example, for a setter in volleyball this might be focusing on the softness of the hands as the ball is received and then released.

- Consider your level of arousal and identify, from past performances, the level of arousal which benefits your performance most.

KEY CONCEPT 5: PLANNING, IMPLEMENTING AND MONITORING TRAINING

PERIODISATION

Recall

Periodisation is the organisation of training into a carefully considered plan which involves different periods of training: the preparation period, the competition period and the transition period. Each period has its own specific aims and purposes.

When you plan a training programme, you must take into account both the nature of the activity and your own role. Some activities, such as competitive swimming, demand more intensive training schedules than, for example, hockey. This is due to the shortness of the competitive season in swimming relative to hockey. In addition, individual fitness requirements require review. For example, the fitness needs of a goalkeeper are very different from those of a midfield player.

DON'T FORGET

For this key concept, you should be familiar with training cycles, their role in performance development and the value to be gained from planning and monitoring your own progress.

PHASES OF TRAINING

The preparation period

The preparation period is based around pre-season training. You start off with general training and progress to more specific training, focusing on improving physical fitness, for example by increasing the intensity of your workouts and decreasing rest intervals. At this point your training programme needs to relate specifically to the nature of the activity and your role within it. Consequently, both skill-related and physical aspects of fitness must be included. You will reap the benefits of your pre-season training work in the next phase: the competition period.

DON'T FORGET

The three main phases of training during a periodised training year are the preparation period, the competition period and the transition period.

The competition period

Your goal during the competition period is to be at your peak of skill-related and physical fitness for the competitions that are most important to you. This is more easily managed if you are, for example, an individual sprinter as opposed to a member of a rugby team. In the former case you have a much greater level of control over your performance. In order to allow you time to complete your physical and mental preparations for competition and avoid the adverse effects of training fatigue, you should 'taper down' your training before competition. After each competition you need to factor in a rest and recovery period. It is ill-advised to begin training again too quickly.

The transition period

The transition period is the phase of training between the competition period and the start of pre-season training. During this period you should not take part in competitions but confine yourself to 'active rest', that is you should maintain a good level of general physical fitness while ensuring that you are rested sufficiently for the demands of pre-season training.

TRAINING CYCLES

Periodisation can be usefully divided into a microcycle, a mesocycle and a macrocycle. These terms describe your training needs over the short term (microcycle), the medium term (mesocycle) and the long term (macrocycle).

- Microcycle generally outlines the training cycle for a specified week of time. The components of the cycle will vary according to your role and the nature of the activity. It will normally include general and specific activity-related forms of training as well as rest periods.

- Mesocycle is the term used to outline your training cycle over a number of weeks, i.e. a set of combined microcycles. For example, a mesocycle can be a month during the preparation period.

- Macrocycle is the term used to describe the overall training period, and would include your training build-up to competitions, tapering down and active rest activities.

LET'S THINK ABOUT THIS

For one activity in your course, explain your training programme for a specified week within a microcycle.

MONITORING PERFORMANCE

Recall

A very important part of a successful fitness training programme is the monitoring of performance. Data on your performance should be collected using the most appropriate method and, after careful analysis, the information should be used to refine your training programme. For example, if the results of your cardio-respiratory endurance test showed that you were not making adequate progress, you could increase frequency and/or duration of your exercises as necessary.

Reviewing your training programme midway can often be useful to collect information relevant to your progress and performance. A review would also allow you to judge if you are likely to meet your targets and make any alterations required.

Finally, it is important that your monitoring of performance considers evidence about your whole performance and not just about your level of fitness. For this reason, it is important that you include information derived from whole performance contexts.

LET'S THINK ABOUT THIS

Choose an activity from your course and explain how you monitored your performance in this activity.

KEY WORDS SUMMARY

Preparation of the Body	Key words
Fitness assessment in relation to personal performance and the demands of activities	standardised procedures, regular monitoring of performance, test norms
Application of different types of fitness in the development of activity-specific performance	performance review, conditioning training
Physical, skill-related and mental aspects of fitness	speed endurance, strength endurance, dynamic strength, local muscular endurance, flexibility, reaction time, agility, balance, movement anticipation, coordination, level of arousal, rehearsal, managing emotions
Principles and methods of training	specificity, progressive overload, intensity, duration, frequency, combined skill and fitness training programmes, adaptation, reversibility
Planning, implementing and monitoring training	identifiable goals, short- and long-term goals, periodisation, peaking for performance, tapering down, phases of training, training cycles, monitoring performance

5 REVIEWING HOW TO ANALYSE YOUR PERFORMANCE: SKILLS AND TECHNIQUES

KEY CONCEPT 1: SKILL AND SKILLED PERFORMANCE

WHAT MAKES A SKILLED PERFORMANCE?

DON'T FORGET

For this key concept, you should be familiar with the criteria required in a skilled performance, the role of the information processing model and the importance of skills and techniques in effective and consistent performance. You should also be aware of the role model performance can play when trying to enhance and develop performance.

Table 5.1 lists features and examples of skilled performance.

Linked movements are performed with **maximum efficiency** and a **minimum of effort**.		In badminton, I practised moving efficiently and in balance to return net shots. I had a wide base of support and low centre of gravity as I lunged to the side. By moving carefully I was able to keep watching the shuttlecock. My non-hitting arm was used to provide balance.
Sequences of movements are carried out in a **fluent**, **controlled** way.		When completing a mid-iron shot in golf, I concentrated on making a smooth controlled, gently accelerating and fluent swing. A well-paced swing in golf assists in generating power.
Correct options are selected; skilled performers perform the right skill at the right time.		As a centre in rugby union, I need to be aware of the options which are available when running in open space. I need to decide whether to retain possession of the ball (carrying the ball either under one arm or in both hands), whether to pass to another player in my team or whether to kick the ball forward either along the ground or a higher kick designed to bounce into touch.

Table 5.1 Features of skilled performance

CHARACTERISTICS OF SKILLED PERFORMANCE

A skilled performance contains many of the characteristics listed in Table 5.2.

Skills and techniques selected reflect the performer's ability and experience. For example, your defending ability in defence at hockey will determine the techniques you can use efficiently and the type of options you can successfully use during games. Your technique and range of options will probably be less extensive than those of players in an international hockey team, but more extensive than those of players new to the activity.		The key to my team's defence is positional ability and experience. As defenders, we try never to face our goal. Instead, we concentrate on remaining between the ball and the goal or between the ball and the shooter. Facing forwards enables us to clear the ball when we gain possession. We try to avoid dribbling as this often leads to penalty corners being conceded through foot contact. Push passing to forward players tends to work better.
Skills are performed consistently. This increases the chances of skills being performed with maximum certainty.		When taking a short corner in hockey I need to be able to consistently pass the ball quickly and accurately to the correct striker. Like many teams, we use predetermined plays. This means that I have to recognise exactly which player in my team to pass the ball towards.
Skilled performance is successful. The right outcome is achieved. Skills have an end result.		As a goal shooter in netball I am expected to score the majority of the points for my team. This involves remaining calm under pressure, focusing on a point at the back of the ring and adding a little backspin to the shot as the ball is released.

Table 5.2 Characteristics of skilled performance

SKILFUL PERFORMANCE: BADMINTON

Table 5.3 lists criteria and qualities of skilled performance in badminton.

Performance criteria		Skilful performance qualities
A broad performance repertoire		Footwork is most effective when movements around the court are economic and efficient. Movement anticipation and reactions are usually accurate and well coordinated. You can show good agility in changing direction quickly. You are competent in most major forehand and backhand shots and are able to show refinement in serving and when playing clear shots to most parts of the court. You can show effective technique when playing a range of underarm and overhead shots. You can play some advanced shots reasonably well, for example, a backhand clear and angled net shots.
Can make appropriate decisions in challenging performance contexts		Can make effective performance decisions in competitive situations which require a range of attacking and defensive options. Can select and combine shots in order to build towards winning rallies. You are able to manoeuvre and outmanoeuvre opponents. You show a reasonable ability to adapt and improvise play when circumstances dictate. You are able to interpret the relative strengths and weaknesses of opponents accurately.
Show control and fluency in performance		Most of the basic hitting skills are automatic and completed with very good control and fluency. Sound preparation, action and recovery are evident with a reasonable degree of technical refinement displayed for more complex shots. Effective performance can be sustained for relatively long periods with quality of shots remaining mostly controlled and fluent when under pressure. Creativity is occasionally apparent through shot selection, definition and/or disguise.

Table 5.3 Skilled performance in badminton

DON'T FORGET

In summary, a skilled performance includes:
- movements which are completed with maximum efficiency and with a minimum of effort
- sequences of movements which are carried out in a fluent, controlled way
- selecting correct options
- selecting skills and techniques according to ability and experience
- performing skills consistently
- performing skills successfully.

LET'S THINK ABOUT THIS

For the activities in your course, identify the different skills and techniques which can indicate that you possess a broad performance repertoire, can make appropriate decisions and show control and fluency in performance.

PROCESSING INFORMATION WHEN LEARNING SKILLS

Recall

When performing in different activities your brain is required to rapidly process information. For example, if during a tennis game your opponent plays a ground shot towards you at 80 km per hour (50 mph) you have a little over 1 second to respond if you are positioned on the baseline.

During this second you need to make decisions about:

- what type of shot is best for returning the ball
- where should the return shot be aimed towards
- what type of spin should be placed on the ball
- where should you move to after playing the return shot?

How can you respond quickly and accurately in such circumstances when you are confronted with so many decisions in such a short time? The answer is that as your performance develops you learn how to process relevant information quickly and effectively.

DON'T FORGET

The information processing model is one method of describing how learning takes place. The information processing approach involves recognising the importance of perception and decision-making. The model is based on the premise that as a stimulus is presented (e.g. a tennis forehand shot) you begin to 'read' the information available and make decisions based on interpreting correctly what to do in a sequential order. The model contains four parts which are linked together in a 'learning loop'.

- The first part of the loop is input information. This is the information you receive from your senses e.g. sight and sound.
- You then make decisions based on the input information you have received. Separating important and less important information is the second part of the loop.
- The third part of the loop is output. This is the way in which you decide to move and respond to the decisions you have made.
- During and after your chosen response you will receive information about your performance. This feedback is the final part of the learning loop.

Information processing model: *Badminton (service reception)*

- **Input:** Position yourself correctly on court to best respond to either a low flick or high serve.

- **Decision-making:** Separate essential from non-essential information. Make a decision about how to return serve and respond.

- **Output:** Return serve and in doing so, try to gain advantage in the rally.

- **Feedback:** Use the quality of returned serve to evaluate your performance and plan changes as necessary. For example, did your return help or hinder you in gaining an advantage in the rally? Did your return link to the type of game plan you are trying to follow? For example, returning a low serve with a low return is trying to play an attacking game with short rallies, while clearing high to the back of the court is more related to a defensive game plan with longer rallies.

LET'S THINK ABOUT THIS

Complete learning loop diagrams for some of the most important skills and techniques included in the activities in your course.

DON'T FORGET

Classification of skills is useful in determining which form of practice suits a particular skill. Categories of skill include: closed or open, simple or complex and discrete/serial or continuous.

CLASSIFICATION OF SKILLS

Closed and open skills

An important concept in skill classification is the open-closed continuum. This means that skills vary between being closed and open. If you are in control of the movement, like the tumble turn in swimming, it is closed. If external forces are in control, as in a game of volleyball or football, it is open.

Open skill example: *Volleyball*

Spiking in volleyball is an open skill due to the number of factors which influence how the spike is completed. The factors include the quality and flight of the set and the number and position of the defending blockers.

Closed skill example: *Swimming*

The tumble turn described on page 10 is a closed skill. To do a tumble turn you follow set movements in order to complete the technique. There are still a few distractions to consider when completing your tumble turn.

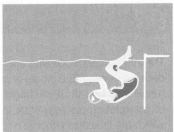

Open and closed skill example: *Trampoline*

Some skills contain both open and closed demands e.g. completing a sequence on the trampoline is essentially a closed skill, however, when completed as part of a team some opens skill demands are involved. These include taking account of your partner's position in the air so that your timing matches each other.

LET'S THINK ABOUT THIS

Try to categorise the skills you have used in the different activities.

SIMPLE OR COMPLEX SKILLS

Skills also vary between simple and complex. Simple skills involve only basic movements and relatively straightforward decision-making. Complex skills are the opposite; they involve making choices between a range of possible decisions and translating the decision into complex or difficult movements.

Whether a skill is simple or complex depends on:

- the number of possible alternative decisions
- the speed at which a decision must be made
- the difficulty of the movement
- the accuracy required of the movement.

contd

SIMPLE OR COMPLEX SKILLS contd

Simple or complex skills: ability considerations
Athletics example (1)

At an introductory level, the skill level required in running a 100 m sprint race is relatively simple. This is because sprinting mostly involves the repetition of set movements and relatively low-level decision-making. However, at an elite performance level, a 100 m sprint race becomes more complex as sprinters have to build up speed from the start, keep the upper body still and relaxed throughout and be aware of other runners without letting them adversely affect the smoothness of their running action. These are complex demands and challenges.

Athletics example (2)

In longer distance running events such as 1500 m, more complex and continuous decision-making is involved than for the 100 m sprinter. This adds to the complexity of the race as runners use feedback about performance during the race to decide on pace judgement and to make decisions about when to try and overtake other competitors and when to begin sprinting for the finish line.

LET'S THINK ABOUT THIS

Consider the level of complexity of the skills involved across the activities in your course and try to categorise those you have encountered so far.

Continuous, discrete or serial skills

Skills can also usefully be classified as discrete skills, serial skills and continuous skills. The table below shows examples of each type of skill and gives a short definition of each.

Continuous skills		**Swimming:** Continuous skills have no clear beginning or end and movements are cyclical or repetitive. Other examples are cycling and running.
Discrete skills		**Goal shooting in netball:** This skill has an obvious and identifiable start and finish point. The skill ends when the shot has been taken. At this point all players become active and make decisions about their court movement and attacking and defensive responsibilities. Other examples are a football kick, tennis serve and golf swing.
Serial skills		**High jump:** Serial skills string discrete skills together correctly. A high jumper must join the approach run, taking off on the correct foot and using the arms and legs to drive the body upwards. This is before arching the back and eventually lifting the legs over the bar. Other examples are dance routines and javelin throwing.

Table 5.4 Examples of continuous, discrete and serial skills.

contd

SIMPLE OR COMPLEX SKILLS contd

Links between closed/open; simple/complex and discrete/serial or continuous skills

Consider the following examples.

Orienteering

Closed: Most of the demands of orienteering are closed. There are few distractions from other performers and other performers have little impact on your own performance. There are, however, some other factors you require to consider when running the course, for example the nature of the terrain. These can usually be understood by studying your map, so orienteering is still predominantly a closed skill.

Complex: The challenges of orienteering are complex. You have to navigate yourself around difficult forest terrain and make effective decisions about which approach to a trig point (marker) is easiest and quickest. You have to complete such tasks while working at a high level of physical intensity.

Serial: While jogging for relaxation would be a continuous skill, orienteering is a serial skill. This is because you tend to follow precise routines for each part of the course. After reaching one trig point you need to study the map, make a decision about how to travel to the next trig point, re-orientate the map, work out how long it will take to reach the next trig point and then start running. When you arrive at the next trig point, you complete the same serial task again.

Gymnastics handspring vault

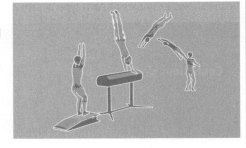

Closed: Completing a handspring is a closed skill as there are few anticipated distractions. You are in control when completing the technique. Within reason, you decide when you are composed enough to begin performance.

Complex: A handspring is a complex technique. Many accurate movements require coordination within a short time. For example, the controlled accelerating run-up has to link to the powerful leg swing to generate rotation.

Serial: The handspring is a serial skill as effective performance is dependent upon different movements linking correctly together. For example, the drive from the arms begins as the legs overtake the hips on the box top. A little delay in beginning the drive is necessary so that flight projects the legs upwards and forwards and not just upwards, which occurs if the drive is too soon.

Netball (centre)

Open: Netball games involve open skills. For a centre, the skills are open because you compete directly against other opponents.

Complex: Most of the skills are complex in netball games as you are competing directly against opponents. If, for some reason, the opposing team placed little pressure on you then passing would become a simpler skill. However, in general, the speed of players' movements and the speed of passing required make the court movement and required passing and catching skills complex.

contd

SIMPLE OR COMPLEX SKILLS contd

Serial: Most of the skills necessary for a centre in netball involve serial skills. Passing involves joining different movements together correctly e.g. protect ball, step forward, transfer weight forward, etc.

Skiing

Closed/Open: This is a difficult skill to classify. Skiing down a constant slope with very few other skiers around in fine weather would be a closed skill. Skiing over different types of terrain with many other skiers around in poor weather would be an open skill. For a ski racer there would be no other skiers on the course and a ski race would usually only take place in reasonable weather, hence closed type skill demands. However, the changing nature of the terrain (ski slope) would make the ski race have some open skill demands as well.

Complex: Ski racing is a complex technique. Many accurate movements require coordination within a short time. Each turn also requires decisions about the degree of turning necessary and the effect this has on the edging and pressuring of the skis.

Serial: Completing a ski race is a serial skill. Effective performance is dependent upon different movements linking correctly together as the end of one ski turn is the beginning of the next turn.

LET'S THINK ABOUT THIS

Using an activity in your course as an example, try to explain whether the skills involved are predominantly open or closed, simple or complex or discrete, serial or continuous.

KEY CONCEPT 2: SKILL/TECHNIQUE IMPROVEMENT THROUGH MECHANICAL OR MOVEMENT ANALYSIS OR CONSIDERATION OF QUALITY — DON'T DO

For this key concept, you should be familiar with at least one of the following three analytical approaches: mechanical analysis, movement analysis or consideration of quality. The nature and demands of activities will often determine which type of analysis will be most beneficial.

MECHANICAL ANALYSIS

Mechanical analysis: *Golf example*

When driving in golf, the effectiveness of the technique can be affected by small parts of the swing. Therefore, completing a mechanical analysis which reviews force, use of body levers and planes of movement would be useful to complete

- **Force:** The greater the force generated through the turning and unwinding of the golf swing combined with the transfer of weight forward, the greater the possibility there is of a long drive.

- **Use of body levers:** The arms combined with the length of the golf club make a long lever for hitting. The force generated by the legs, hips and upper body as they turn needs to be transferred to the long lever.

- **Planes of movement:** All movement of the body can be broken down into three basic planes of movement: sagittal, frontal and transverse. In the golf drive, the turning and transfer of weight from the rear to front foot involves movement across the sagittal plane to generate force.

Mechanical analysis: *Hurdling example*

Analysis of hurdling technique is often completed by a mechanical analysis of force and resistance. Maintaining a streamlined body shape as you run and cross the hurdle means that force generated by driving backwards against the ground can overcome the resistance provided by the height of the hurdle and other possible factors, e.g. running into a headwind.

Action/reaction

All analyses of the mechanics of movement are based on the physical laws. Fundamentally, all muscle-powered movements follow Newton's Third Law of Motion, i.e. for every action there is an equal and opposite reaction. For example, as the sprinter drives backwards and downwards onto the blocks, there is an equal and opposite upwards and forwards reaction.

MOVEMENT ANALYSIS

Recall

Movement analysis breaks down the performance of an activity into its component parts. The observation schedule on page 10 analyses the sequence of preparation, action and recovery movements involved in completing a tumble turn in swimming. This form of analysis can reveal correctable flaws and errors in specific movements or parts of the performance. It can therefore be very useful when analysing the effectiveness of particular techniques.

contd

MOVEMENT ANALYSIS contd

In some activities, such as dance and gymnastics, it is preferable to use effort factors (time, weight, space and flow) when collecting information through movement analysis. These factors can be more suitable for analysing aesthetic performances.

CONSIDERATION OF QUALITY

Recall

The different performance qualities highlighted in Chapter 3 (Performance Appreciation) – technical, physical, personal and special – are frequently used as criteria for analysis of performance. The nature and demands of different activities and your role within activities will determine which of these criteria is the most appropriate.

In gymnastics, top performers have the ability to control movements precisely as well as performing in public with expression, flair and creativity. If you wanted to analyse performance using this example, considering the performance qualities of control, refinement and effectiveness alongside those of expression, flair and creativity would be beneficial.

 ## LET'S THINK ABOUT THIS

Consider the various analytical approaches you have undertaken in your course and why different approaches were more effective for certain activities.

NEW TECHNOLOGIES AND THE ANALYSIS AND DEVELOPMENT OF PERFORMANCE

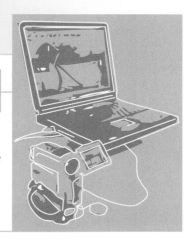

The observation schedule shown on pages 9 and 10 are completed with pencil and paper. In future years, it is likely that new technologies will play an increasing part in data collection. Computer software packages are already available which allow digital recordings of performance to be analysed on screen. This enables you to immediately view your performance and make split screen comparisons with model performers. Networked computers make it possible for a whole class of students to follow teacher explanations about performance and performance improvement. Self-study tasks could follow such lessons.

 www.dartfish.com and www.quintic.com

PLANNING FOR PERFORMANCE IMPROVEMENT USING MECHANICAL, MOVEMENT OR CONSIDERATION OF QUALITY ANALYSIS

Example: The tumble turn observation checklist on page 10 could demonstrate the use of these three analytical approaches in planning. The checklist has two self-check boxes. This will enable you to review your progress and monitor improvements in your performance.

DON'T FORGET

If using new technologies has been part of your course then you should make sure that you mention these learning experiences in your assessment answers.

KEY CONCEPT 3: THE DEVELOPMENT OF SKILL AND THE REFINEMENT OF TECHNIQUE

PREPARATION STAGE

Recall

During this stage, you find out the main components of the skill (often called subroutines). You are gathering information about each part of the skill and starting to perform each part. You need not necessarily be a novice in the activity. For example, a dancer has to learn new routines, for which they may have to go through a preparation stage. During this stage, you will make many errors and your skill level will be low. You will need to have the active encouragement and support of your coach or teacher to ensure that you stay motivated and make effective progress.

At the preparation stage of learning skills, demonstrations with verbal explanations are often used to show how skills and techniques are performed. For example, in swimming your teacher may often demonstrate the angle at which your hand and arm should enter the water when explaining the arm action required in front crawl swimming.

The preparation stage: *Volleyball (spiking)*

- You become familiar with the basic idea of how to 'spike'.

- You gradually get used to running forwards and transferring weight upwards.

- You get used to a two-footed take-off and hitting the ball with a single arm movement.

- You make quite a lot of errors – you often travel forwards after jumping and your hitting action lacks control and fluency.

- The spike often travels in different directions.

- You receive advice from teachers/friends.

LET'S THINK ABOUT THIS

Considering your own performance in an activity, select a preparation skill and try to describe the role that skill played in your performance progression.

PRACTICE STAGE

Recall

During this stage, you start to join all of the movements or subroutines together, e.g. a gymnast who is completing a handspring or a handstand forward roll in its complete form is at the practice stage of skill learning. The length and frequency of your practice sessions will depend on your aptitude, level of fitness, motivation and past experience, as well as the complexity of the skill. Relatively easy to perform skills (handstand forward roll) will need less practice than complex skills (handspring). This is because refining the precision of the movements required is more complex, as is recognising where errors exist.

Practising effectively will reduce performance errors and improve the precision with which movements are executed. At the practice stage of skill learning, feedback is required for showing you what to do next rather than for explaining what has just happened.

The practice stage: *Volleyball (spiking)*

- The spike becomes more fluent as the hitting action is mostly completed at the highest part of your jump.

- There are fewer errors – the jump and hitting action are more controlled and the spike is becoming more accurate, although some further refinement is still necessary.

- You become less reliant on teacher advice and are able to evaluate your own performance.

LET'S THINK ABOUT THIS

Considering your own performance in an activity, select a practice skill and try to describe the role that skill played in your performance progression.

AUTOMATIC STAGE

By this stage of skill learning you will be able to execute most key subroutines automatically. Consequently, you pay little attention to them as you can sequence and time subroutines effectively. An example of the automatic stage in volleyball spiking is given below.

At the automatic stage of skill learning you are making fewer errors and you are able to rely on your own internal feedback rather than the external feedback supplied by teachers and other students.

The automatic stage: *Volleyball (spiking)*

- The spike action is becoming fluent and precise as the hitting action is smooth and consistent.

- The arm is taken fully back during the jump in anticipation of the spike.

- There are very few errors or inconsistencies in the spike action.

- As most of the spike action has become automatic, you now have the chance to pay selective attention to other aspects of the spike action e.g. you can observe closely where your opponents are standing and vary where your spike is directed towards.

- You have become less reliant on teacher advice and are able to evaluate, through internal feedback, which specific aspects of your service action require improvement.

Considering your own performance in an activity, select an automatic skill and try to describe the role that skill played in your performance progression.

PRACTICE METHODS

Solo/shadow/partner/group

Realistic practice is crucial and there are several useful approaches that will help you to undertake the most focused practice possible to ensure your level of performance improves.

Solo/shadow/partner/group: *Table tennis*

Solo practice is possible in table tennis and often works best when you half the table space. This allows practice to play continuously as the ball rebounds off the vertical half of the table. Playing a variety of shots against the table enables you to establish the pattern of the movements and the subroutines involved in playing different shots.

Shadow practice: This method, which can add progression to your practice, consists of shadowing (mirroring) another player who is completing identical movements. Shadow practice makes you concentrate on the other player's movements as you execute the same movements yourself. This can help you to appreciate the flow of movements required as you attack and defend in rallies. These types of practices often begin without using a table tennis ball at all, but as your skill level improves the demands of practices increase. Playing cooperative movement-based practices involving actual rather than imagined stroke play allows skill development.

Partner practice: In this type of practice you can usefully introduce training intervals, e.g. you might work cooperatively together with your partner on set hitting routines. This could involve practising set forehand to backhand hitting routines which require you to react, move and hit in precise ways and to be alert. **Progression** could be added by including practice variation which involves hitting backhand to backhand and such like.

Group practice: Further progression can often be added to partner practices to make practices increasingly demanding for example through practising set forehand to backhand hitting routines as part of a doubles team. This type of group practice requires additional cooperation and more refined movement and hitting.

Considering the various forms of practice you have undertaken, select a particular activity and try to describe the benefits gained from engaging in focused practice.

contd

PRACTICE METHODS contd

Opposed/unopposed

Recall

The strength of your opposition is critical in game situations. Therefore, altering the strength of the opposition can be a very useful practice method. Practices can be described as having no opposition, passive (limited) opposition and active (full) opposition.

- Practising with **no opposition** is usually done at the **preparation stage**.
- Practising with **limited opposition** is usually done at the **practice stage**.
- Practising with **active opposition** is usually done at the **automatic stage**.

In order to ensure that your practice is effective, it is very important that the other player or players are working to an agreed level of opposition.

 LET'S THINK ABOUT THIS

Can you explain when you have used opposed/unopposed practices on your course?

Gradual build-up

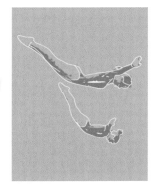

With the gradual build-up method of practice, you master each skill before moving on to the next. This is good for building confidence as your goals should be challenging but achievable. This method is good if you are learning complex skills. It is also an effective method for practising skills with an element of risk. By using gradual build-up, you can increase the difficulty of each practice by a small amount to ensure practices become gradually more demanding.

Complicated sequences of movements can be developed **in stages** by gradually increasing the demands of the practice. For example, in trampolining this could be achieved either by practising longer sequences of your routine or by practising more difficult combinations within the routine, or by a combination of both approaches.

 LET'S THINK ABOUT THIS

Can you explain when you have used gradual build-up practices on your course?

Repetition practices

Repetition practices involve breaking the technique into its component parts and practising these individual parts repeatedly. These practices can also involve repeating the entire technique. Your goal is to refine the technique so you move seamlessly from one part to another. This method of practice is especially effective with **complex, closed skills** such as a tennis serve or a golf swing.

LET'S THINK ABOUT THIS

Can you explain when you have used repetition practices on your course?

contd

Drill practices

The best drills involve repetition under varying degrees of pressure.

The aim of the following drills practice is to encourage players to practise moving sideways – left and right – before playing a volley return in volleyball. Two helpers stand 5 m apart and feed the ball forward for the practising player to volley and return. Then they move sideways for 5 m in balance and receive and return another volley. This can be continued for another few occasions before rest. This drill could be completed as part of a simple warm-up. However, progression could be added by making the drill part of a skills circuit. Rotation with the two feeders would allow a 1:2 work to rest ratio. Progression could also be added by making the drill more technically demanding. For example, it could be that you receive a forward pass but require volleying a diagonal return to the opposite helper and vice versa. It could also be that the feeders could feed the ball more quickly, making it necessary that the sliding sideways steps be completed quicker while still retaining good dynamic balance when moving.

LET'S THINK ABOUT THIS

You should be able to explain when you used drill practices on your course.

Massed/distributed practice

In deciding whether to have massed (continuous) practice or distributed (spaced) practice, the following should be considered:

- where the skill lies along the simple-complex continuum

- the motivation, experience and aptitude of the performer

- whether practice is likely to leave the performer fatigued.

Massed practice is not generally used with beginners (preparation stage of skill learning) due to the likelihood of fatigue occurring and performance suffering as a result.

Distributed practice is more effective when the technique being practised is complex.

Massed practice: *Swimming*

The aim of effective swimming is to maintain your technique and speed while becoming increasingly tired (fatigued). Therefore, continuous massed practice would benefit you as swimming in a technically proficient way and at a regular speed makes the practice challenges close to those experienced when competing in swimming.

Distributed practice: *Modern dance*

Distributed short practice would work well if you were completing a complex dance sequence based around performing a number of contrasting movements. If performance is continuous there is a risk of injury if you become too tired. Therefore, a few practice attempts of specific movements combined with rest intervals would be best. During rest intervals mental rehearsal training could help you to focus on the qualitatative aspects of how movements were emphasised and completed.

LET'S THINK ABOUT THIS

Can you explain when you have used massed or distributed practices on your course?

contd

PRACTICE METHODS contd

Conditioned games/small-sided games/coached games

It is often helpful to practise different forms of games when you are learning and developing open skills, as these can reproduce the requirements of full competitive games.

Conditioned games can be constructed in different ways and are frequently used to give one side an advantage over the other in order to make achieving tasks or performing skills easier.

Example 1: In different directly competitive games, you can often limit the number of touches players take on the ball to establish whether skills are controlled and fluent when under pressure. For example, in football you can play conditioned games were players can only take a maximum of three touches of the ball.

Example 2: You can change the formal rules in conditioned games in order to emphasise specific skills and techniques you have been practising previously. In hockey, for example, often each team can defend and attack two goals in the same conditioned game. The goals would be placed on usual goal line but be placed midway between the centre and side of the pitch. Playing under these conditions can emphasise the importance of width and mobility in attack and defence.

 LET'S THINK ABOUT THIS

Can you explain when you have used conditioned games on your course?

Small-sided games: In small-sided games the number of players in the teams is reduced. This gives each individual player greater opportunities for practising their skills and techniques. It is important that small-sided games reflect the demands of competitive matches and that players are performing at the correct level of their ability.

Coached games: In coached games your coach or teacher will halt the game or activity in order to make particular suggestions for improvement or highlight examples of good practice

LET'S THINK ABOUT THIS

Try to explain when you have used small-sided and/or coached games on your course.

Whole/part/whole

In order to obtain the benefit from the whole/part/whole practice method, some experience of the activity is required. You need to be able to at least attempt a version of the whole skill. Understanding the components of different skills and techniques will determine whether whole/ part/whole is a feasible practice method or not. Skills which can be isolated and practised individually are most suited to this method. Whole/part/whole is not an effective method for practising continuous skills.

Volleyball: When spiking in volleyball, you may have difficulty avoiding travelling forwards when you jump up high to spike. If you touch the net, this counts as a rule infringement and your team loses the point. Practising running forward for a few steps and jumping up may be useful before returning to a volleyball game in which the whole spiking action is used.

LET'S THINK ABOUT THIS

You should be able to explain when you have used whole/part/whole as a practice method on your course.

PRINCIPLES OF EFFECTIVE PRACTICE

For practice to be effective, it should:

- have clear and achievable objectives
- be specific to improving your skill and technique weaknesses
- avoid becoming overlong and repetitive, as this will affect your level of motivation as well as leading to tiredness and fatigue
- be interesting and enjoyable
- be based on your existing level of ability.

Work/rest ratio

Setting the correct work/rest ratio is important in tailoring your fitness programme to your specific requirements. The work to rest ratio in any practice situation will depend on:

- the performer's previous experience
- the performer's ability level
- the physical demands included in practices
- the difficulty of the skill involved.

Practising under pressure

- With skills and techniques that you can complete with a high degree of control and fluency (automatic stage of skill learning) it is important to practise when under pressure.
- This will make practices **realistic** and similar to when you perform them in competition. In team activities, this could involve increasing the demands of opposition during practice.
- Practising under pressure can also involve individual activities such as swimming e.g. when completing sets of 100 m front crawl timed swims you might practice with another swimmer beside you. This makes practice closely match the demands of full performance situations.

LET'S THINK ABOUT THIS

You should be able to explain when you have practised skills and techniques under pressure on your course.

Progression

In order to achieve effective progression in an activity:

- practices should be based on the performer's current level of ability
- performers should recognise that high-quality practice for short periods of time is most effective
- performers should avoid the adverse effects of boredom and fatigue (in swimming, for example, you can alter the strokes to make practice more interesting and enjoyable).

How long to practise for?

Another principle of effective practice is that you practice for a suitable **training time**. Too short a time means that improvements will be limited. Too long a practice session and you may become fatigued and prone to injury. Training for too long a time can also lead to boredom and a gradual reduction in the amount of progress you make.

The correct training time will depend upon the demands of the activity. For activities such as swimming and for longer distance running events in athletics, training times are usually long. For other activities, such as throwing and sprinting events in athletics, training times tend to be shorter.

DON'T FORGET

When planning practices three vital considerations are the work/rest ratio you set, how you organise practising under pressure and how progression is added to your practices.

contd

PRINCIPLES OF EFFECTIVE PRACTICE contd

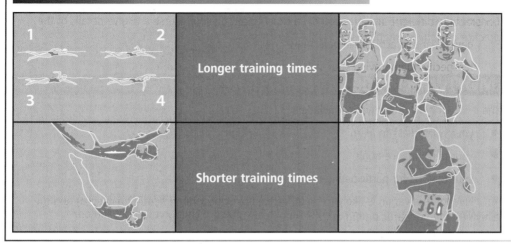

LINKING STAGE OF SKILL LEARNING TO PRINCIPLES OF EFFECTIVE PRACTICE

Table tennis

The diagram below shows three examples of how you could match your current level of performance and stage of skill learning with the design principles for developing effective practices in table tennis.

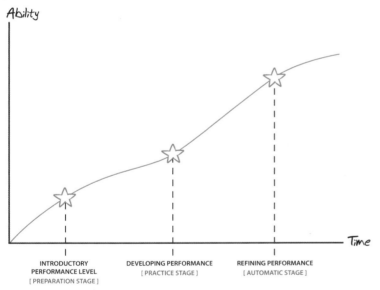

INTRODUCTORY
PERFORMANCE LEVEL
[PREPARATION STAGE]

DEVELOPING PERFORMANCE
[PRACTICE STAGE]

REFINING PERFORMANCE
[AUTOMATIC STAGE]

Shadow practice:
Practicing court movement routines.

Partner practice:
Practicing set hitting routines.

Recall

The principles of effective practice are as follows.

- Practices need clear and achievable objectives.

- Practices need to be specific to your skill and technique weaknesses.

- Practices need to be interesting and enjoyable.

- Practices need to be based on your existing level of ability.

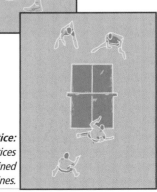

Group practice:
Partner practicing to make practices increasingly demanding. Refined movement and hitting routines.

Consider the different activities you have experienced on your course and give details of the practice objectives you have set.

MOTIVATION, CONCENTRATION AND FEEDBACK

The **components** of motivation include:

- your willingness to learn
- your performance goals
- your reasons for participating in different activities.

Your level of motivation is likely to be influenced by your commitment (persistence) and the activities you are participating in.

Motivation can be either **internal** (intrinsic) or **external** (extrinsic).

Internal Motivation is your own 'will to win'. This is always an important factor in any sporting activity. The best performers in both amateur and professional sport require very high levels of internal motivation to constantly train and work at skills.

External Motivation is when you take part in an activity for reasons other than the simple enjoyment of participation. If your reason for participation is to earn money this would be an example of external motivation. External motivation seldom occurs in physical education and sport. Even highly paid football, tennis and golf professionals also have high levels of internal motivation.

LET'S THINK ABOUT THIS

Can you explain your level of internal and external motivation for the different activities in your course?

Motivation: Individual differences

- Your level of motivation for different activities is likely to be **different** from other classmates.
- Your may prefer team-based sports and performing in a competitive pressured situation.
- You may enjoy most individual activities with closed skills that are not directly competitive, where you enjoy the concentration and attention to detail required.
- Levels of motivation will vary both within a class and within a team: every individual has an optimum level of motivation. Elite performers can control their level of motivation to optimise performance.

LET'S THINK ABOUT THIS

You should be able to explain what optimum level of motivation means for you in one activity on your course.

contd

MOTIVATION, CONCENTRATION AND FEEDBACK contd

Goal-setting

Goal-setting: *Tennis*

Your target could be to try and improve the percentage of first serves which are successful. For example, setting a target of 60% of serves to be completed as first serves. If you achieve this target consistently in competitive matches you could reset the target to, for example, achieving a target of 70% of serves to be completed as first serves. This planned approach to goal setting ensures that the confidence you gain from achieving your goals can be included in the setting of future targets.

DON'T FORGET

You cannot perform at the highest level without setting yourself challenging goals and targets for specific aspects of your performance.

Concentration

During an activity, high-level performers pay closer attention to some factors than others.

Lapses in concentration often occur due to tiredness e.g. repeatedly conceding goals in the last few minutes of games. Therefore, to improve your teams defending, it would be useful to practise when you are already tired as this would make practice as realistic as possible.

Anxiety is another cause of lapse of concentration. Anxiety can lead to you paying attention to the wrong aspects of performance. For example, in a 1500 m race paying too much attention to other runners can limit your ability to concentrate on your performance. Therefore, to improve your performance it would be useful to focus more on running your own race and less on how other runners are running their races.

DON'T FORGET

Concentration is the ability to focus on the most important parts of your performance and block out other less relevant task cues.

Concentration: *Rugby Union* (open skill)

When you are completing an attacking move in rugby you need to pay attention to the movement of the ball, the movements of your team mates and movements of the players in the opposing team. When you receive a pass you need to decide quickly what to do: whether to pass, kick or continue running with the ball. In making your decision, you need to correctly identify which factors to pay most attention to and those which are not as essential to concentrate on. For example, if you decide to continue passing the ball along the three-quarter line to other team mates, then it is usually less necessary to continue paying attention to those players who were involved in passing before you received the ball.

LET'S THINK ABOUT THIS

Choose one open skill from an activity on your course. Explain the performance factors you paid full and partial attention towards.

Concentration: *Gymnastics* (closed skill)

When performing a twisting vault in gymnastics you need to pay full attention to the degree of control and definition in certain parts of the techniques (e.g. the quarter aerial rotation, the push off from the horse, the continuing rotation and stretching out to lengthen the flight) and less attention to other more routine aspects of your sequence, such as your run approach. This occurs because you are able to focus your attention on the most important parts of your twisting vault and pay less attention to other more routine parts of the vault.

contd

LET'S THINK ABOUT THIS

Consider a specific open skill related to an activity on your course and give details of the performance factors you were required to scrutinise fully and partially.

Concentration and level of ability

At a beginner level (preparation stage of skill learning) you are unable to focus on many aspects of performance at the same time. Instead, you need to focus nearly all of your concentration on the basic aspects of performance. As your performance improves (practice stage of skill learning), it is only necessary for you to pay selective attention to some of the simple parts of your performance as by now you can manage these parts with the required control and fluency.

Concentration and selective attention

Your level of concentration must meet the requirements of the activity. In general, it is difficult to pay full attention all the time. You therefore raise your concentration levels at special times and lower your concentration levels as intensity of play decreases, e.g. in tennis in the seconds between rallies when you have time to briefly relax and focus on the next point. As you prepare to serve or receive service, your level of attention then increases so that you are concentrating fully as the point begins.

Feedback

> **DON'T FORGET**
>
> Feedback is the information others give you after observing your performance.

- As you learn from your experience, you store feedback information in your memory and recall it as necessary.

- The types of feedback you need will vary depending on the nature of the tasks and skills required by the activity.

- Feedback should be constructive and give specific pointers to how performance can be improved.

- Effective feedback is positive rather than negative. It should focus on what was good about a performance while indicating where improvements could occur.

There are two types of feedback

- **Internal (intrinsic) feedback** centres on the performer's self-awareness of the good and bad points of their movements and actions and how well they feel they have performed. Internal feedback is often referred to as 'kinaesthetic awareness'.

- **external (extrinsic) feedback** comprises information from observers (teachers, coaches and team mates), knowledge of results, observation schedules, factors affecting results and a video of performances. External feedback should be given as soon as possible after the activity or task is completed and should give targeted information on the performance.

Internal and external feedback: *Tennis*

In tennis, when completing a low backhand volley you receive internal feedback about the action through the control of the racquet and through your dynamic balance, co-ordination and timing when completing the volley. When completing a low backhand volley you also receive external feedback based on the outcome of the volley (i.e. was a point won or not) and when your teacher provides you with information about the aspects of the technique which led to a successful or unsuccessful volley.

contd

MOTIVATION, CONCENTRATION AND FEEDBACK contd

Internal and external feedback: *Basketball*

Internal feedback

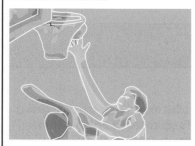

In basketball when completing a lay up shot, you receive internal feedback about the action by sensing how well controlled the run up was, the quality of the jump and how well the shooting action was completed. Consequently, you are able to develop a feeling and awareness of whether the lay up shot was effective or not. For the same action, you could also use different forms of external feedback. You could use a digital recording of your lay up shot to analyse the main factors that affected your performance. This could supply you with information about whether or not the ball was laid carefully onto the backboard and whether the ball was protected from defenders as you completed your jumping and shooting action.

External feedback

LET'S THINK ABOUT THIS

Give two examples of internal and external feedback from one activity in your course.

External feedback: Knowledge of results

A particularly useful form of external feedback is knowledge of results, especially in competitive matches when play moves too fast to allow you to analyse your own performance.

Knowledge of results: *Rugby union*

Knowledge of results information can go beyond mentioning the outcomes of a game and describe the frequency and effectiveness of how different skills and techniques within the game were performed, as demonstrated in Table 5.5.

Team A		Team B
75	Passes completed	66
60	Tackles made	54
16	Tackles missed	23
8	Scrums won on put-in	7
1	Scrums lost on put-in	4
12	Lineouts won on throw	9
1	Lineouts lost on throw	4
12	Turnovers won	9

Table 5.5 Knowledge of results example

Links between feedback and motivation

Feedback and motivation are often best considered together. For example when your coach gives you positive feedback on your performance, your motivation will increase. Remember that the opposite is also true, so be careful not to give negative feedback to team mates!

Links between feedback and goal-setting

Positive feedback is also beneficial to consider when goal-setting. If your goal is to retain your balance on the beam, positive feedback (both internal and external) will benefit your performance and be helpful in securing your optimum level of motivation.

DON'T FORGET

Link stages of learning, methods of practice, principles of effective practice and the study of motivation, concentration and feedback together. This enables coherent practice.

KEY WORDS SUMMARY

Skills and techniques	Key words
The concepts of skill and skilled performance	fluent controlled movements, selecting correct options, skills which reflect experience and ability, information processing, learning loop, decision-making, open and closed skills, simple and complex skills, discrete/serial and continuous skills, variations in technique
Skill/technique improvement through mechanical analysis, movement analysis or consideration of quality	force, body levers, planes of movement, preparation, action and recovery, managing effort factors in performance, personal and technical qualities
The development of skill and the refinement of technique	preparation, practice and automatic stages of learning, solo/shadow/partner/group practice, opposed/unopposed practice, repetition/drills practice, massed/distributed practice, conditioned games/small-sided games, whole/part/whole practice, work to rest ratios, progression, internal motivation, goal setting, external motivation, concentration, forms of feedback, knowledge of results, effect of boredom and fatigue

6 REVIEWING HOW TO ANALYSE YOUR PERFORMANCE: STRUCTURES, STRATEGIES AND COMPOSITION

KEY CONCEPT 1: STRUCTURES, STRATEGIES AND/OR COMPOSITIONAL ELEMENTS FUNDAMENTAL TO ACTIVITIES

STRUCTURES AND STRATEGY

Structures (for example a 4-4-2 football formation) and strategy (the management and application of tactics) in any game of movement revolve around (i) how to create space for your attacking manoeuvres and (ii) how to deny space to your opponents during the periods when you must defend. Structures and strategy can and should be analysed in detail and prepared before the match, i.e. you should have a game plan.

Structures and strategy: Individual activity (singles game of table tennis)

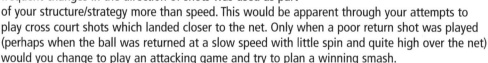

If the structure and strategy you chose was to play an attacking game, this would involve you trying to play at a fast pace (tempo) and forcing your opponent back from the table so that they were required to play defensive shots from deep positions. This would help you in trying to win points.

If the structure and strategy you chose was to play a defensive game, then you would be trying to play a shorter game where frequent changes in the direction of shots was used as part of your structure/strategy more than speed. This would be apparent through your attempts to play cross court shots which landed closer to the net. Only when a poor return shot was played (perhaps when the ball was returned at a slow speed with little spin and quite high over the net) would you change to play an attacking game and try to plan a winning smash.

Structures and strategy: Team activity (football)

You can also try to control the tempo of a football game to suit your team strengths. If the structure and strategy you wanted to play was an attacking game, then you would try to play at a fast pace by attacking as quickly as possible. This could involve trying to push your full backs ahead of the midfield players and creating an overlap in attack which might be difficult for the opposing team to defend against, due to the increased range of options available to your team.

STRUCTURES AND COMPOSITION

The essentials of structures and composition centre on the creative character of the performance. These are of key importance (e.g. in dance), and include the elements below.

- Design considers how to use space effectively to develop different themes and combinations.
- Form considers how a dance or gymnastics routine is constructed. This might be done through the use of different themes or combinations, e.g. rondo, canon, binary or ternary.
- Style includes types of dance.

KEY CONCEPT 2: IDENTIFICATION OF STRENGTHS AND WEAKNESSES IN PERFORMANCE

ROLES AND RELATIONSHIPS

Recall

It is vital to the success of any team or group of players that each individual understands their responsibilities (e.g. attacking and defensive responsibilities). You also must be aware of how your role relates to the other members of the team or group. The individual role you adopt will be dependent on many factors e.g. your physical attributes and your decision-making qualities. After reviewing individual strengths and weaknesses, it is possible for suitable structures and strategies or structures and composition to be planned.

Roles and relationships: *Volleyball*

The six players in a volleyball team must all rotate position (clockwise) every time their team wins service from the opposing team. Players have specialist positions for attack and defence and the success of any strategies adopted will be dependent upon how well the team operates as a **unit**, with each player performing **his/her own role** to the best of their ability. In attack, only the three players at the net positions can jump and spike or block near the net (left forward, setter and right forward). In defence, the three backcourt players (left back, centre back and right back) can only hit the ball over the net if they jump from behind the attack line (the 3 m line) which separates the front and back part of the court. Substitutions are allowed during the game.

LET'S THINK ABOUT THIS

You should be able to explain your roles and responsibilities for one activity in your course.

FORMATIONS

DON'T FORGET

Analysing the effectiveness of width, depth and mobility within your strategy helps you to plan when and how to adapt your formation.

Recall

The most effective formations will reflect the strengths and weaknesses of the team or group and its individual members. You can then either refine your chosen formation or use another formation if your team's performance is less than you expected.

LET'S THINK ABOUT THIS

Explain the formation you used in one activity in your course.

Formations: *Hockey examples*

Four popular formations (described in Table 6.1) are 1-3-3-3, 2-3-5, 4-2-4 (the numbers referring to the defenders, midfield players and attackers in a team) and the W-M formation. The main differences are **positional**. For example, in a 1-3-3-3 formation you have an extra defender in comparison to a 2-3-5 formation, as you have three players playing in deep defence instead of two in the 2-3-5 formation. The 2-3-5 formation is an attacking formation as you have five as opposed to three attacking players in the 1-3-3-3.

contd

FORMATIONS contd

Formation	Strengths	Weaknesses	Diagram
1-3-3-3	• fluid (mobile) system of play as 3 midfield players can support attackers and defenders as necessary • the single sweeper in defence can cover opposing players who get beyond the three defenders	• midfield players require high levels of cardio-respiratory endurance to support attackers and defenders as necessary • long passing more difficult due to the distance possible between defence, midfield and attack	GOALKEEPER, SWEEPER, RIGHT BACK, CENTRE BACK, LEFT BACK, MIDFIELD, MIDFIELD, MIDFIELD, STRIKER, STRIKER, STRIKER
2-3-5	• the links between the three midfield and five attacking players are helped by two of the attacking players dropping a little deeper to help link play • supports a fast open attacking game plan which has a good balance between width, depth and mobility in attack	• when opposing teams are attacking there is often space available in the wide areas of the pitch • midfield players are required to get back in numbers and help defend	GOALKEEPER, RIGHT BACK, LEFT BACK, RIGHT HALF, CENTRE HALF, LEFT HALF, RIGHT WING, INSIDE RIGHT, CENTRE FORWARD, INSIDE LEFT, LEFT WING
4-2-4	• when the right and left backs get forward they can usefully support the midfield and attacking players as overlapping full backs if they are fast and mobile players • width is provided both in defence and attack, effectively creating a 2-4-4 when attacking and a 4-4-2 when defending	• when opposing teams are attacking there is often space available in the wide areas around the middle area of the pitch • forward players are required to get back in numbers and help defend	GOALKEEPER, RIGHT BACK, CENTRE BACK, CENTRE BACK, LEFT BACK, MIDFIELD, MIDFIELD, STRIKER, STRIKER, RIGHT WING, LEFT WING
W-M	• when defending the centre half (number 5 player) can drop back a little deeper to help provide greater depth in defence by marking the oppositions centre forward • the centre of midfield can become a strong part of both defensive and attacking play when players are mobile and communicate effectively with each other	• when opposing teams are attacking there is often space available in the wide areas of the middle of the pitch • the defending (W) players can become rather isolated from the attacking (M) players and vice versa	1, 2, 5, 3, 4, 6, 8, 10, 7, 5, 11

Table 6.1 The strengths and weaknesses of 4 popular hockey formations

contd

Adapting a formations strategy: *Hockey*

One adaptation possible within a 1-3-3-3 formation is for the sweeper to move forward and ahead of the three defenders. The formation becomes a 3-1-3-3 with the sweeper more clearly supporting the midfield and attacking players in the team than previously. This change to formation could be a good idea if your team were doing well and were able to commit to playing a more attacking game

Formations: *Dance*

The qualities of cooperation, support and effective communication are also important in formations. Within dance, it is beneficial if those in your group are receptive to new ideas and can work well with others (cooperation and support) as effective communication helps with the constructive development and presentation of a performance.

TACTICAL ELEMENTS

Recall

Tactics can be defined as the particular ways in which you implement a strategic plan. Tactics are designed to optimise your team's strengths while taking advantage of the other team's weaknesses. The choice of tactics will often be influenced by the score and the time remaining to play.

Tactical elements: *Volleyball*

Different defensive strategies are often used in volleyball. The decisions about what type of defence to use can be reviewed as the game progresses and changed if necessary.

In the picture, the defending team is placing two blockers at the net to try and defend against the opposing team's attack. This leaves the remaining four players in the team to cover the remainder of the court and defend as necessary. However, a number of factors might persuade the defending team to change their tactic as the game progresses.

For example, if the opposing team is very good at attacking you might decide to just place a single blocker at the net so that another defender is able to try to retrieve the spike. Alternately, the score in the game might dictate that a further change of tactic was required. So, you might consider trying to block at the net more aggressively by adding a third blocker when possible. This might mean that a blocked spike could drop on the attackers' side of the net with a point being quickly won. You might also adopt this tactic if you consider that the attacking team is poor at spiking in general.

LET'S THINK ABOUT THIS

Try to explain the tactical elements you have considered and adapted within one activity on your course.

DESIGN ELEMENTS

Recall

The overall design, form and style are especially significant elements in dance performances and floor work in gymnastics.

Design

The overall design in a performance includes compositional considerations about the different movements included in your gymnastics routine. For example, you can usually enhance your performance by varying the movements to include your full repertoire of techniques and by making changes in the way some familiar movements are repeated. For example, it might be better if your routine includes two dive forward rolls to make the first one particularly high with a relatively slow open roll and the second with a faster tighter roll.

Form

Form involves reviewing how a performance is structured. In a gymnastics sequence, you review how well the performance space is covered and the different directions of travel which are included in your performance.

Style

The style emphasised within a gymnastics floor sequence varies according to the type of music which is used to accompany the performance. The music creates a mood, an atmosphere which you try to reflect in your movements throughout the routine.

CHOREOGRAPHY AND COMPOSITION

Timing, precision and improvisation in performance are key considerations in choreography and composition. Reviewing them will help you to prepare your presentation in order to maximise its effect on the audience in terms of technical skill, aesthetic and emotional appeal and overall appreciation of your performance. It is important to be able to improvise in order to expand and develop your repertoire of steps and movements.

KEY CONCEPT 3: INFORMATION PROCESSING, PROBLEM-SOLVING AND DECISION-MAKING WHEN WORKING TO DEVELOP AND IMPROVE PERFORMANCE

INFORMATION PROCESSING, PROBLEM-SOLVING AND DECISION MAKING

DON'T FORGET

In some activities, more time is available for decision-making than in others. What kinds of decisions you make often depends on whether the skills involved in the activity are open or closed and on the time available for making effective decisions.

Making effective decisions under pressure: *Football*

In football, improving strategic decision-making effectiveness is an important quality to develop as players are required to anticipate ball direction instead of watching the ball and then making decisions about where to move. As well as anticipating ball direction, expert players can observe and respond to the patterns of play occurring by observing the movements of players who are moving 'off the ball'.

To improve the process of making effective decisions under pressure, it is necessary that practices and small-sided games reflect the demands of full competitive games. This can often occur best by having practices and games which focus on cooperative attacking and follow particular defensive systems of play so that players can become accustomed to following set strategies and set-plays.

LET'S THINK ABOUT THIS

Explain how effective your individual/team/group decision-making has been using an activity from your course. Explain the effects upon your performance when you were required to perform under pressure.

KEY WORDS SUMMARY

Structures, strategies and composition	Key words
The structures, strategies and/or compositional elements that are fundamental to activities	tempo, deception, design form and style with a composition
Identification of strengths and weaknesses in performance in terms of roles and relationships, formations, tactical or design elements and choreography	support, continuity, pressure, improvisation, cohesion, width, depth, mobility, systems of play, positive team/group ethos, interpreting stimulus, timing, improvisation
Information processing, problem-solving and decision-making when working to develop and improve performance	adapting and refining, individual and group decision-making, dynamics and relationships

PERFORMANCE DEVELOPMENT

The third stage in the cycle of analysis, following on from investigation and analysis, is developing your performance.

PLAN OF ACTION

The first part of developing your performance is to plan a course of action. It is important that the chosen course of action links effectively with the information you have collected about your performance and is related to the key concepts in the specific area of analysis and development of performance you are developing.

- In Performance appreciation (Chapter 3), this could involve linking your collected data on how you managed your emotions during a competition with your analysis of factors influencing the planning and management. This would allow a plan of action to be produced, which is designed to improve your managing of your emotions in ever more demanding performance contexts.

- In Preparation of the body (Chapter 4), this could involve linking your collected data on your fitness test scores with your analysis of the principles and methods of training to produce a plan of action designed to make fitness training more specific to your performance needs in activities.

- In Skills and techniques (Chapter 5), this could involve linking your collected data on comparisons with a model performer with your analysis of the development of skills and techniques to produce a plan of action which links more coherently to your stage of skill learning.

- In Structures, strategies and composition (Chapter 6), this could involve linking your collected data on the effectiveness of a strategy within a game with your analysis of problem-solving and decision-making in games to produce a plan of action which aims to improve your appreciation of the factors which can influence problem solving and decision-making in games.

MONITORING YOUR PERFORMANCE

The second part of developing your performance is to monitor your performance. Progress should be monitored frequently and your plan of action altered according to the results. Feedback gained from monitoring your performance can inform your decision making when reviewing your goals. During your course you will have collected information about your performance (stage 1 of the cycle of analysis. This data should be continually referred to when monitoring your performance to enable you to compare past performances with current performances.

With specific regard to the four examples from the different areas of analysis and development of performance mentioned above this, this could involve the following.

- In Performance appreciation (Chapter 3), this could involve monitoring your performance by reviewing how well you managed your emotions in ever more demanding performance contexts.

- In Preparation of the body (Chapter 4), this could involve monitoring whether any adaptations to your training programme were effective.

- In Skills and techniques (Chapter 5), this could include monitoring how well the methods of practice chosen were appropriate for your stage of skill learning.

- In Structures, strategies and composition (Chapter 6), this could include monitoring how well strategic challenges arising in games were addressed.

EVALUATING YOUR PERFORMANCE

Evaluating your performance is the fourth and final key step in the Cycle of Analysis. After you have collected information about your performance, related it to selected key concepts and explained how you developed your performance, you then evaluate your performance.

When you evaluate your performance, make sure that your review includes both specific and general aspects of performance. For example, when reviewing the effectiveness of your putting in golf, analyse the effectiveness of your putting technique as well as considering how putting influenced your overall golf performance.

Specific putting performance	General game performance	Match results

LET'S THINK ABOUT THIS

In evaluating your performance improvements try to link them to the performance abilities which are required within the performance unit i.e. repertoire of skills and techniques, effective decision-making and control and fluency. If you can make these performance connections, it will help add to the depth and quality of performance review.

Repertoire of skills and techniques	Effective decision-making	Control and fluency

PERFORMANCE APPRECIATION

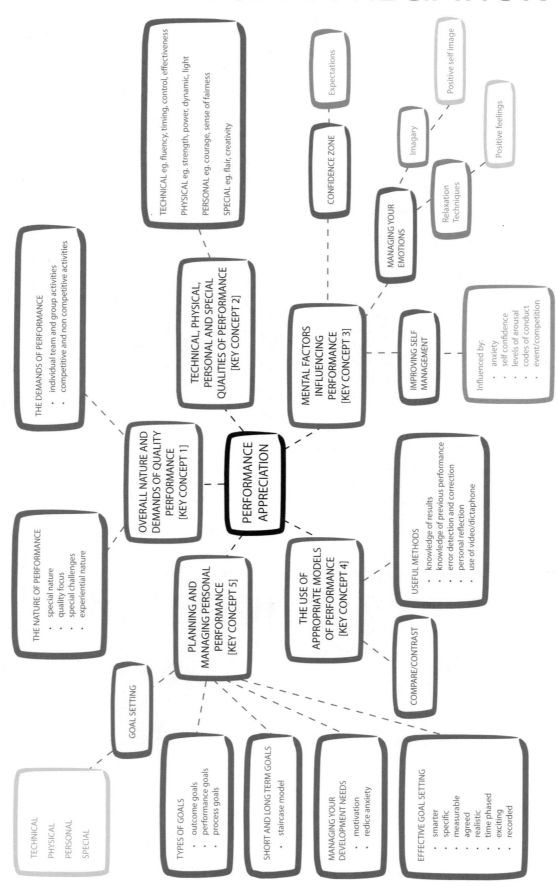

THE DEMANDS OF PERFORMANCE
- individual team and group activities
- competitive and non competitive activities

TECHNICAL eg. fluency, timing, control, effectiveness

PHYSICAL eg. strength, power, dynamic, light

PERSONAL eg. courage, sense of fairness

SPECIAL eg. flair, creativity

TECHNICAL, PHYSICAL, PERSONAL AND SPECIAL QUALITIES OF PERFORMANCE [KEY CONCEPT 2]

Expectations

Positive self image

Imagary

CONFIDENCE ZONE

Positive feelings

Relaxation Techniques

MANAGING YOUR EMOTIONS

MENTAL FACTORS INFLUENCING PERFORMANCE [KEY CONCEPT 3]

IMPROVING SELF MANAGEMENT

Influenced by:
- anxiety
- self confidence
- levels of arousal
- codes of conduct
- event/competition

OVERALL NATURE AND DEMANDS OF QUALITY PERFORMANCE [KEY CONCEPT 1]

PERFORMANCE APPRECIATION

USEFUL METHODS
- knowledge of results
- knowledge of previous performance
- error detection and correction
- personal reflection
- use of video/dictaphone

THE NATURE OF PERFORMANCE
- special nature
- quality focus
- special challenges
- experiential nature

PLANNING AND MANAGING PERSONAL PERFORMANCE [KEY CONCEPT 5]

THE USE OF APPROPRIATE MODELS OF PERFORMANCE [KEY CONCEPT 4]

COMPARE/CONTRAST

GOAL SETTING

TECHNICAL

PHYSICAL

PERSONAL

SPECIAL

TYPES OF GOALS
- outcome goals
- performance goals
- process goals

SHORT AND LONG TERM GOALS
- staircase model

MANAGING YOUR DEVELOPMENT NEEDS
- motivation
- redice anxiety

EFFECTIVE GOAL SETTING
- smarter
- specific
- measurable
- agreed
- realistic
- time phased
- exciting
- recorded

PREPARATION OF THE BODY

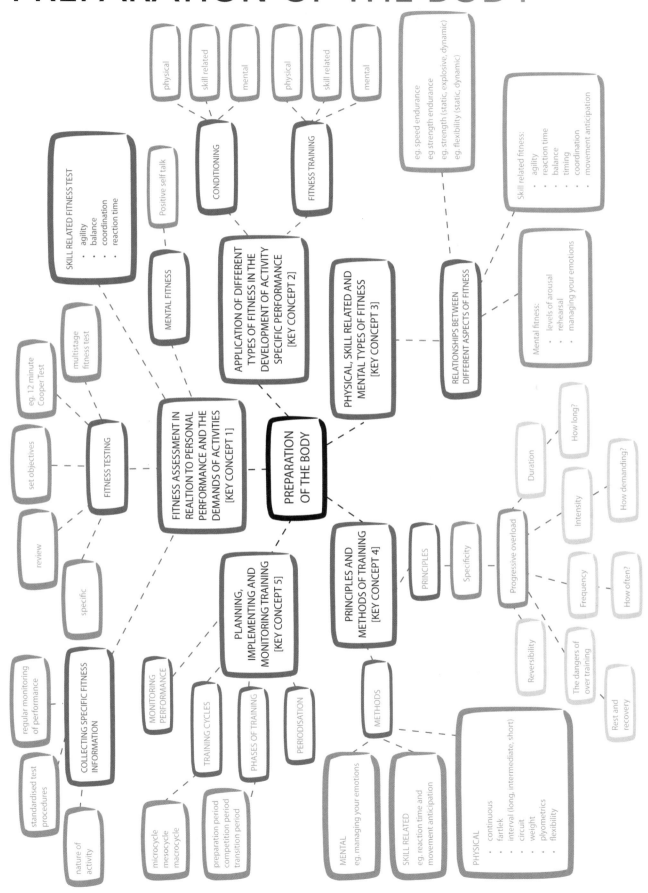

SKILL RELATED FITNESS TEST
- agility
- balance
- coordination
- reaction time

physical

skill related

mental

physical

skill related

mental

eg. speed endurance
eg strength endurance
eg. strength (static, explosive, dynamic)
eg. flexibility (static, dynamic)

Skill related fitness:
- agility
- reaction time
- balance
- timing
- coordination
- movement anticipation

CONDITIONING

FITNESS TRAINING

Positive self talk

MENTAL FITNESS

APPLICATION OF DIFFERENT TYPES OF FITNESS IN THE DEVELOPMENT OF ACTIVITY SPECIFIC PERFORMANCE [KEY CONCEPT 2]

PHYSICAL, SKILL RELATED AND MENTAL TYPES OF FITNESS [KEY CONCEPT 3]

RELATIONSHIPS BETWEEN DIFFERENT ASPECTS OF FITNESS

Mental fitness:
- levels of arousal
- rehearsal
- managing your emotions

multistage fitness test

eg. 12 minute Cooper Test

FITNESS TESTING

set objectives

review

FITNESS ASSESSMENT IN REALTION TO PERSONAL PERFORMANCE AND THE DEMANDS OF ACTIVITIES [KEY CONCEPT 1]

PREPARATION OF THE BODY

How long?

How demanding?

How often?

Duration

Intensity

Frequency

Progressive overload

PRINCIPLES

Specificity

PRINCIPLES AND METHODS OF TRAINING [KEY CONCEPT 4]

specific

regular monitoring of performance

COLLECTING SPECIFIC FITNESS INFORMATION

MONITORING PERFORMANCE

PLANNING, IMPLEMENTING AND MONITORING TRAINING [KEY CONCEPT 5]

TRAINING CYCLES

PHASES OF TRAINING

PERIODISATION

METHODS

Reversibility

The dangers of over training

Rest and recovery

standardised test procedures

nature of activity

microcycle
mesocycle
macrocycle

preparation period
competition period
transition period

MENTAL
eg. managing your emotions

SKILL RELATED
eg. reaction time and movement anticipation

PHYSICAL
- continuous
- fartlek
- interval (long, intermediate, short)
- circuit
- weight
- plyometrics
- flexibility

SKILLS AND TECHNIQUES

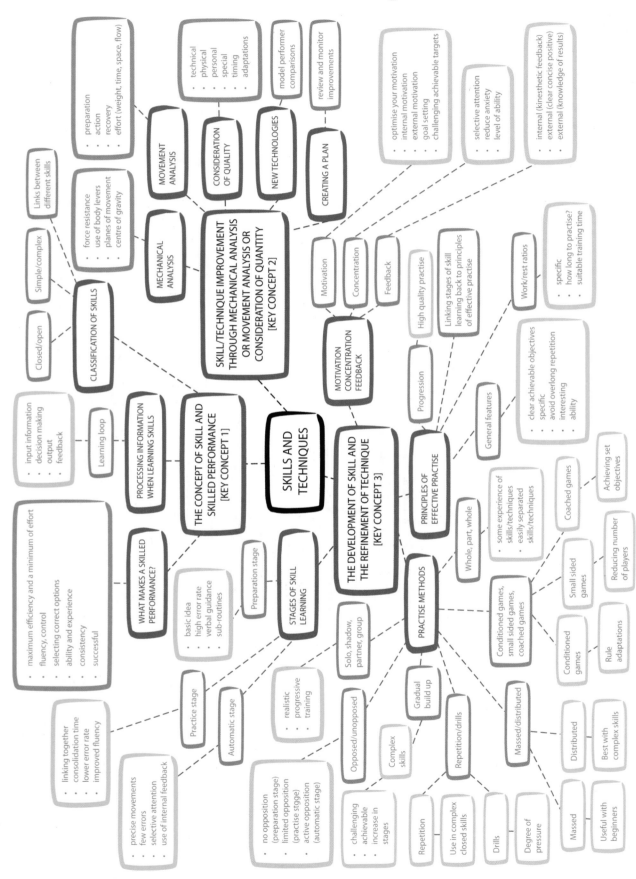

SKILLS AND TECHNIQUES

THE CONCEPT OF SKILL AND SKILLED PERFORMANCE [KEY CONCEPT 1]

SKILL/TECHNIQUE IMPROVEMENT THROUGH MECHANICAL ANALYSIS OR MOVEMENT ANALYSIS OR CONSIDERATION OF QUANTITY [KEY CONCEPT 2]

THE DEVELOPMENT OF SKILL AND THE REFINEMENT OF TECHNIQUE [KEY CONCEPT 3]

PROCESSING INFORMATION WHEN LEARNING SKILLS

- input information
- decision making
- output
- feedback

Learning loop

CLASSIFICATION OF SKILLS

Closed/open

Simple/complex

Links between different skills

MOVEMENT ANALYSIS

- preparation
- action
- recovery
- effort (weight, time, space, flow)

MECHANICAL ANALYSIS

- force resistance
- use of body levers
- planes of movement
- centre of gravity

CONSIDERATION OF QUALITY

- technical
- physical
- personal
- special
- timing
- adaptations

NEW TECHNOLOGIES

- model performer comparisons

CREATING A PLAN

- review and monitor improvements

- optimise your motivation
- internal motivation
- external motivation
- goal setting
- challenging achievable targets

- selective attention
- reduce anxiety
- level of ability

- internal (kinesthetic feedback)
- external (clear concise positive)
- external (knowledge of results)

MOTIVATION CONCENTRATION FEEDBACK

Motivation

Concentration

Feedback

High quality practise

Linking stages of skill learning back to principles of effective practise

Work/rest ratios

- specific
- how long to practise?
- suitable training time

Progression

General features

- clear achievable objectives
- specific
- avoid overlong repetition
- interesting
- ability

PRINCIPLES OF EFFECTIVE PRACTISE

Whole, part, whole

- some experience of skills/techniques
- easily separated skills/techniques

Coached games

Achieving set objectives

Small sided games

Reducing number of players

PRACTISE METHODS

Conditioned games, small sided games, coached games

Conditioned games

Rule adaptations

WHAT MAKES A SKILLED PERFORMANCE?

- maximum efficiency and a minimum of effort
- fluency, control
- selecting correct options
- ability and experience
- consistency
- successful

STAGES OF SKILL LEARNING

Preparation stage

- basic idea
- high error rate
- verbal guidance
- sub-routines

Practice stage

Automatic stage

- linking together
- consolidation time
- lower error rate
- improved fluency

- precise movements
- few errors
- selective attention
- use of internal feedback

Solo, shadow, partner, group

Gradual build up

- realistic
- progressive
- training

Opposed/unopposed

Complex skills

Repetition/drills

Massed/distributed

- no opposition (preparation stage)
- limited opposition (practise stge)
- active opposition (automatic stage)

- challenging
- achievable
- increase in stages

Repetition

Use in complex closed skills

Drills

Degree of pressure

Distributed

Best with complex skills

Massed

Useful with beginners

STRUCTURES, STRATEGIES AND COMPOSITION

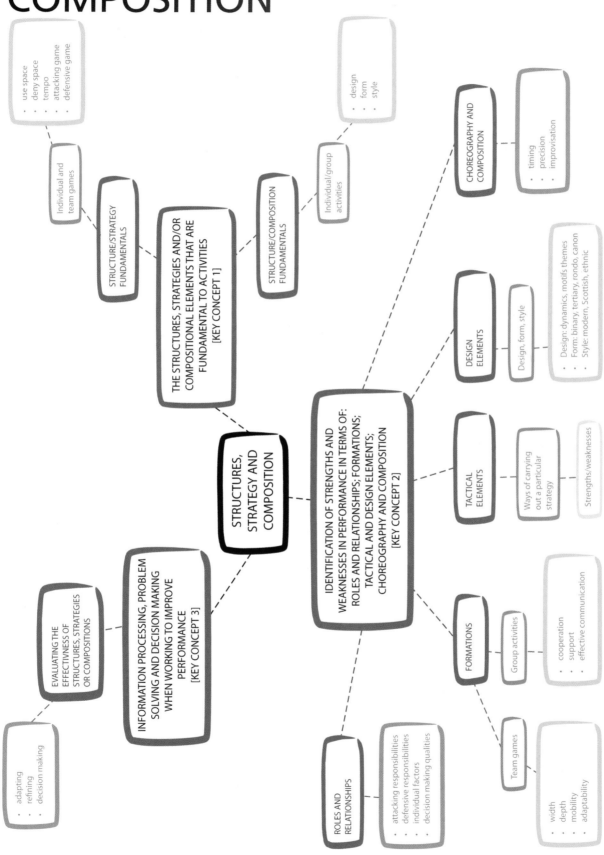

STRUCTURES, STRATEGY AND COMPOSITION

THE STRUCTURES, STRATEGIES AND/OR COMPOSITIONAL ELEMENTS THAT ARE FUNDAMENTAL TO ACTIVITIES [KEY CONCEPT 1]

STRUCTURE/STRATEGY FUNDAMENTALS

Individual and team games

- use space
- deny space
- tempo
- attacking game
- defensive game

STRUCTURE/COMPOSITION FUNDAMENTALS

Individual/group activities

- design
- form
- style

CHOREOGRAPHY AND COMPOSITION

- timing
- precision
- improvisation

IDENTIFICATION OF STRENGTHS AND WEAKNESSES IN PERFORMANCE IN TERMS OF: ROLES AND RELATIONSHIPS; FORMATIONS; TACTICAL AND DESIGN ELEMENTS; CHOREOGRAPHY AND COMPOSITION [KEY CONCEPT 2]

DESIGN ELEMENTS

Design, form, style

- Design: dynamics, motifs themes
- Form: binary, tertiary, rondo, canon
- Style: modern, Scottish, ethnic

TACTICAL ELEMENTS

Ways of carrying out a particular strategy

Strengths/weaknesses

FORMATIONS

Group activities

- cooperation
- support
- effective communication

Team games

- width
- depth
- mobility
- adaptability

ROLES AND RELATIONSHIPS

- attacking responsibilities
- defensive responsibilities
- individual factors
- decision making qualities

INFORMATION PROCESSING, PROBLEM SOLVING AND DECISION MAKING WHEN WORKING TO IMPROVE PERFORMANCE [KEY CONCEPT 3]

EVALUATING THE EFFECTIVENESS OF STRUCTURES, STRATEGIES OR COMPOSITIONS

- adapting
- refining
- decision making

INDEX

INDEX